or more than 25 years, The Institute of Internal Auditors has looked to The Research Foundation to define leading internal audit practices and to promote the profession to academic institutions. The Foundation's board of trustees recently redefined their mission as:

> *"To be the recognized leader in sponsoring and disseminating research, to assist and guide internal auditing professionals and others, in the areas of risk management, controls, governance processes and audit practices."*

The Research Foundation is committed to:
- Defining internal auditing practices as performed by global leaders in research reports.
- Educating practitioners, educators, and the general public about the merits of internal auditing.
- Distributing materials on the benefits of internal auditing to organizational leaders and clients.

To continue to benefit from this ongoing effort and to help The Foundation fund top-quality research studies and educational programs for internal auditors worldwide, join the Master Key Program. For $1,000, your organization can become a subscriber and receive all Research Foundation publications and research reports as soon as they come off the press.

2001 Master Key subscribers will receive titles like:
- *An e-Risk Primer*
- *Independence and Objectivity: A Framework for Internal Auditors*
- *Internal Auditing Reengineering: Survey, Model, and Best Practices*
- *Enterprise Risk Management: Trends and Emerging Practices*
- *Effective Compliance Systems*
- *Fraud and Its Deterrence*
- *Value Added Services of Internal Auditors*

To subscribe to the Master Key Program, call: +1-407-830-7600, Ext. 279 or
e-mail: research@theiia.org

*Count on The IIA Research Foundation to help you perfect
your profession and empower your success. Subscribe today.*

To order individual copies of Research Foundation reports:
Online: www.theiia.org under The IIA
E-mail: iiapubs@pbd.org

ENTERPRISE RISK MANAGEMENT:
TRENDS AND EMERGING PRACTICES

Prepared by Tillinghast - Towers Perrin

Tillinghast - Towers Perrin

Principal Authors
Jerry A. Miccolis, Kevin Hively, and Brian W. Merkley

With the assistance of

The Conference Board of Canada
Le Conference Board du Canada

The Institute of Internal Auditors Research Foundation

With Sponsorship by:
Entergy Services, Inc.
Southern Company Services, Inc.
Wal-Mart Stores, Inc.

ISBN 0-89413-458-2
01161   07/01
First Printing

CONTENTS

The Institute of Internal Auditors Research Foundation

The Institute of Internal Auditors Research Foundation

LIST OF FIGURES AND TABLES

Figures

The Institute of Internal Auditors Research Foundation

The Institute of Internal Auditors Research Foundation

The Institute of Internal Auditors Research Foundation

Tables

ABOUT THE ORGANIZATIONS

THE INSTITUTE OF INTERNAL AUDITORS RESEARCH FOUNDATION

In 1976, The Institute of Internal Auditors (IIA) established a Research Foundation as a separate corporate entity for purposes of education and research in internal auditing. The IIA Research Foundation's mission is to be the recognized worldwide leader in sponsoring and disseminating research on risk management, control, and governance processes. The Institute of Internal Auditors is headquartered in Altamonte Springs, Florida, and has more than 73,000 members in more than 120 countries.

TILLINGHAST – TOWERS PERRIN

Tillinghast – Towers Perrin provides management consulting to financial services organizations worldwide. Their clients include banks, investment managers, securities firms, and insurance organizations. In addition, their risk management practice consults to a wide range of organizations beyond the financial services industry. Their consultants help clients improve business performance through quantitative analysis, insight, and execution. They work with clients to develop strategies that are tailored to their needs.

Tillinghast - Towers Perrin is part of Towers Perrin, one of the world's largest independent consulting firms, with over 9,000 employees in more than 20 countries. Towers Perrin helps organizations improve business performance through people, advising them on human resource management, employee benefits, compensation, communication, strategy, and organizational effectiveness. For more information, please visit www.towers.com.

THE CONFERENCE BOARD OF CANADA

The Conference Board of Canada is an independent, not-for-profit applied research institution whose mission is to help its members anticipate and respond to the increasingly changing global economy. This is accomplished through the development and exchange of knowledge about organizational strategies and practices, emerging economic and social trends, and key public policy issues. For more information, please visit www.conferenceboard.ca.

ABOUT THE PRINCIPAL AUTHORS

Jerry A. Miccolis is a risk management consultant and consulting actuary with Tillinghast - Towers Perrin in its Parsippany office. He is a principal of Towers Perrin.

Mr. Miccolis is architect of several of Towers Perrin's multidisciplinary service offerings, including workers' compensation cost management, strategic risk financing, and, currently, enterprise risk management. He has served in a number of practice leadership positions, including practice leader for the worldwide risk management practice. He is a widely quoted speaker and author on risk management issues.

Mr. Miccolis' client responsibilities include managing consulting engagements with the firm's large corporate clients. His work has included workers' compensation cost management, total health management, strategic risk financing, enterprise risk management, loss forecasting, financial modeling, funding analysis, and general management consulting. He also has undertaken actuarial and management consulting assignments with traditional and captive insurance companies and statutory insurance funds, and has worked with legislators and regulatory authorities, providing advice, including expert witness testimony, on proposed insurance legislation/regulations, financial examinations, and rate filings.

A Fellow of the Casualty Actuarial Society and a member of the American Academy of Actuaries, Mr. Miccolis has served both groups on a number of professional committees, chairing several, and sitting on the Casualty Committee of the Actuarial Standards Board. He currently chairs the CAS Advisory Committee on Enterprise Risk Management. Mr. Miccolis also has authored and reviewed/refereed professional papers in the actuarial literature and has served as an editor of CAS and Towers Perrin publications. He holds a B.S. in mathematics from Drexel University.

Prior to joining Tillinghast in 1980, Mr. Miccolis was associated with the Chubb Corporation, where he managed the Actuarial Research and Development Department, which was responsible for the development of new products and pricing methodologies.

The Institute of Internal Auditors Research Foundation

Kevin Hively is a managing consultant with the Towers Perrin Business Performance Practice. Mr. Hively's strategic advisory work has included business planning, market research, transaction support, and industry analyses.

Examples of recent strategy projects include:

- Strategic review of the global cancer burden for a leading public health organization.
- Due diligence review for a private placement investment into a B2B energy Internet auction site.
- Creation of the Internet content distribution strategy for a leading public health education and research organization.
- Competitive analysis of business model design and global sales and marketing structure in the PC industry for a Fortune 100 IT company.
- Market analysis and company valuation of acquisition target for a global building materials manufacturer.
- Strategic review of domestic multisource business for a global pharmaceutical company.
- Assessment of product feasibility for a venture capital investment in a wireless communications company.
- Creation of the business plan for a new retail power marketing joint venture.

Mr. Hively is a member of the Towers Perrin Enterprise Risk Management team. He published "Revisiting Your Organization" in the July 1998 issue of *Integrated Energy Investor.*

Before joining Telesis, Mr. Hively was director of policy for the governor of the state of Rhode Island where he was responsible for planning and policy development. In that role he led the governor's effort to deregulate the electricity industry. Prior to Mr. Hively's service in state government, he served as policy director for RIPEC, a policy and fiscal advisory body created by the state's largest companies.

Mr. Hively served on the review panel for the Slater Technology Fund — a public/private seed capital program in Rhode Island. He has also been a member of national working committees for the American Enterprise Institute and the Aspen Institute. He is a graduate of Brown University.

Brian W. Merkley served as the project coordinator in the development of this publication. He is a risk management consultant with Tillinghast - Towers Perrin in its Dallas office. Prior to joining Tillinghast, he worked for several years as a project manager for a national consulting firm that specializes in measuring and managing environmental, health, and safety risks.

At Tillinghast, Mr. Merkley has undertaken a variety of risk management assignments with a focus on enterprise risk management (ERM), strategic risk financing, and risk management information systems (RMIS). His recent project involvement includes:

- Enterprise-wide risk assessment project for a major health insurer.
- Captive feasibility and strategic benefits financing study for a leading international manufacturer.
- Risk financing and risk program reviews for a variety of clients, including a major U.S. university, a U.S.-based health care provider, and a steel manufacturer based in Latin America.
- Process assistance to several clients that are implementing new RMIS.
- Evaluation of environmental-related exposures for a large non-profit organization.
- Analysis of environmental remediation costs for a multinational electronics firm involved in merger and acquisition.

Mr. Merkley has spoken on the subject of ERM at international conferences and recently authored the article, "Does Enterprise Risk Management Count?," published in the April 2001 issue of *Risk Management*.

Mr. Merkley earned his B.S. degree at Brigham Young University and his M.B.A. from the University of Georgia with concentrations in risk management, insurance, and finance. He is a member of the Global Association of Risk Professionals (GARP) and holds the Associate in Risk Management (ARM) professional designation.

The Institute of Internal Auditors Research Foundation

ACKNOWLEDGMENTS

We appreciate the support of The Institute of Internal Auditors Research Foundation (IIA RF), especially Roland Laing, former Manager of Research, and Susan Lione, Senior Manager of Research. We also would like to thank the individual members of the Board of Research Advisors who worked so closely with us on this project. They provided valuable insight and perspectives during our several meetings and during the manuscript review process. We especially would like to thank Frank Tallerico of Pioneer Hi Bred International for leading the committee and Rod Winters of Microsoft for his service as the executive champion for this project.

We wish to acknowledge the assistance of The Conference Board of Canada, especially Karen Thiessen, Program Manager and Researcher. Karen coordinated the surveying of her organization's members and also led the effort to produce the Hydro-Québec case study.

We are grateful to Dr. Robert Hoyt of the Center for Enterprise Risk Management (CERM) at The University of Georgia for his help with developing the survey content and for his assistance with the literature review. We also wish to acknowledge Felix Kloman, Editor of *Risk Management Reports*, for his review of the survey questionnaire.

We wish to thank the organizations that responded to the survey and to the organizations that are featured as case studies in this book. We are grateful for the willingness of so many individuals at these organizations to share their time with us and relate their experiences with respect to enterprise risk management.

Many of our colleagues at Tillinghast – Towers Perrin provided valuable advice and assistance to us throughout this project. We are grateful for their contributions and wish to acknowledge them:

- Gwen Ezell of Hartford for her assistance on the literature search and review.
- Dave Finnis of Sydney for his help with facilitating the survey and conducting the case study with the Australian communications company discussed in the book.
- Joe Langan of Dallas for his assistance with designing and conducting the survey and for his input during the analysis of the survey responses.
- Chuck Lee of Dallas for his thorough review of the manuscript as well as his extensive contributions in several key areas that helped us shape this book.
- Julian Phillips of London for his many efforts associated with the survey and the development of the case studies on Bradford & Bingley, Holcim and Infineon.

- Helene Pouliot of Toronto for her assistance with the Clarica case study.
- Sae Wi of Providence for his assistance in the gathering of the initial bibliography and conducting secondary research on the topic.
- Samir Shah of Washington, D.C., John Yonkunas of Hartford, and Laura Thumel of Chicago, for their assistance with survey design and content.

Finally, the project would not have been completed without the efforts of our administrative assistants, Judy Robinson, Raeanne Alves, and Colleen French.

EXECUTIVE SUMMARY

Objectives and Approach to the Study

The Institute of Internal Auditors Research Foundation and Tillinghast - Towers Perrin, with the assistance of The Conference Board of Canada, undertook this study to help answer the following questions:

- What is meant by "Enterprise Risk Management" (ERM)?
- What is the current state of ERM across various industries?
- Who is doing ERM? Why? What results have they achieved?
- What tools, techniques, and processes are available to implement ERM?
- What is the future of ERM?

The study comprised a literature review, a custom-designed multi-industry survey, and interviews with a number of leading organizations in ERM. Based on the results of this research and accumulated knowledge from Tillinghast - Towers Perrin's client experience, this report presents our perspective on trends and emerging practices in ERM.

Summary Results

Current State

Defining ERM

Definitions of ERM abound, but they generally differ more in form than in substance. The important characteristics of most sound definitions are:

- Inclusion of risks from all sources (financial, operational, strategic, etc.) and exploitation of the "natural hedges" and "portfolio effects" from treating these risks in the collective.
- Coordination of risk management strategies that span:
    - Risk assessment (including identification, analysis, measurement, and prioritization).
    - Risk mitigation (including control processes).
    - Risk financing (including internal funding and external transfer such as insurance and hedging).
    - Risk monitoring (including internal and external reporting and feedback into risk assessment, continuing the loop).

The Institute of Internal Auditors Research Foundation

- Focus on the impact to the organization's overall financial and strategic objectives.
- Recognition of the upside, as well as the downside, nature of risk.

In the Introduction, we offer a definition of ERM that captures these characteristics.

What's Different About ERM?

ERM differs considerably from "traditional" risk management. Traditionally, risk management has been focused more narrowly in terms of scope of risks, types of risk management strategies, and the impact and nature of risk. The scope traditionally has been confined to purely hazard, or property/liability, risks, and the strategies have concentrated on insurance solutions, primarily. As a result, the traditional approach has tended to treat risk as a strictly downside phenomenon, and the focus has been not on the impact on the organization's bottom-line objectives, but on the risks that lend themselves to an insurance solution, regardless of materiality.

The Current State of ERM

Quite a number of organizations — large and small, across varied industries — are undertaking ERM. Their motivations range from external pressure (e.g., corporate governance guidelines, regulations, institutional investor concerns) to sound business practice to competitive advantage. Many have developed new tools and metrics. Some have successfully integrated ERM with other processes such as internal auditing and strategic planning. None acknowledge having completed the process. The "ERM movement" is still in its early years, but clearly already has its very strong adherents. Some of their stories are related in the case studies included in this report.

Results from Benchmarking Survey

In late 2000, we conducted a multi-industry global survey of chief financial officers, chief audit executives, chief corporate counsels, and chief risk officers to better understand the issues surrounding ERM. Our analysis of the survey results indicates the following:

- A desire for a unifying framework and corporate governance regimes are key drivers of ERM.
- Earnings growth and revenue growth are the top business issues today and will continue to be three years from now, and earnings consistency is expected to grow in importance.
- Organizations view ERM as a tool to help manage their most important business issues.
- ERM tends to be found among larger organizations.
- ERM is still in its earliest stages of application, but few respondents to the survey are ignoring it.

- Senior executives lead ERM activities and internal auditing plays a substantial role in implementing ERM.
- Organizational barriers need to be overcome to implement ERM.
- Comprehensive risk assessments exist in few organizations.
- ERM may initially be more of a management information tool than a driver of corporate performance.
- A variety of tools and metrics are used.

We discuss each of the major survey results listed above in Chapter 1 and provide more detail and analysis of the survey results in Chapter 2.

Success Factors and Lessons Learned

Our interviews with several leading organizations in ERM, summarized as case studies in Chapters 3 through 10, and our other research suggest that some of the important drivers of success in ERM are:

- Having strong and visible support from senior management (e.g., CEO, CFO, CRO).
- Having a dedicated group of cross-functional staff to drive ERM implementation and continue to push it in its operational phase.
- Closely linking ERM to the key strategic and financial objectives of the organization and to the business planning processes.
- Introducing ERM as an enhancement to already entrenched and well-accepted processes within the organization, rather than as a new, stand-alone process.
- Importing ideas from the outside.
- Proceeding incrementally and leveraging "early wins."

Summary Analysis

ERM is clearly a management tool coming into increasing vogue throughout a number of industries such as energy, manufacturing, and financial services. Over the next several years, internal discussions on ERM are likely to increase with internal auditing playing a key role in these discussions.

As organizations move forward with ERM, they need to consider a number of items:

- Which conceptual model of ERM will be used and what adaptations will be necessary to meet the organization's needs?
- How will it be rolled out within the organization, e.g., geographically, by organizational unit, key functions?

The Institute of Internal Auditors Research Foundation

- How "deep" is senior management's support?
- What tools and metrics should be employed?
- Will ERM be used as a management information tool or as a performance driver?
- Should ERM be linked to compensation and incentive design?
- How should ERM be communicated to stakeholders, if at all?

Implementing ERM

It is fair to say that no two organizations are taking the same route to ERM. Most are proceeding incrementally. Some are beginning by layering additional sources of risk, one at a time, into their existing processes for assessment, mitigation, etc. Some are embracing all sources of risk at the outset, but are tackling the processes one at a time, with most starting with risk assessment. Others are taking on all risk sources and all processes, but on a small, manageable subset of their operations as a "pilot project." Most all are seeking "early wins" that will help build momentum and promote further development toward their ideal ERM process. We believe the detailed survey results and the case study descriptions in this report provide useful material to organizations looking for implementation guidance, including the types of things they should have in their toolboxes.

The Future of ERM

Beyond the objective observations cited above, we can offer our prognostications on where ERM is headed. It seems clear that ERM is more than another management fad or buzzword of the moment, and more than an academic theory. Organizations with a reputation for good management are often those doing ERM before their peers. We believe ERM will become an integral part of the management process for organizations of the 21st century. It will influence how organizations are structured, with some appointing a chief risk officer that reports to the CEO or board of directors. It will influence how strategic planning is done. And it will certainly influence how internal auditing is performed.

INTRODUCTION

Earlier this year *The Wall St. Journal* reported about the impact of a fire on the business fortunes of mobile phone manufacturers Nokia and Ericsson[1]. A factory fire at a key independent supplier of chips for handsets to both organizations closed down the chip factory causing shipments of chips to halt. How Nokia and Ericsson responded set the stage for a dramatic change in the global battle for mobile phones.

Based on published reports, Nokia acted quickly and activated a crisis management plan that allowed production to continue relatively unabated. In contrast, Ericsson was caught unprepared and unable to respond quickly enough to protect its market position.

Viewed another way, one organization's fire (a traditional hazard risk) became two other organizations' strategic dilemma. The end result is a tale of two very different fortunes:

- Nokia increased market share at the expense of Ericsson and cemented its lead in mobile handsets.
- Ericsson lost potentially $400 million in revenue (although some of that will be made up through insurance claims), but more importantly lost strategic ground in the mobile phone battle. Ericsson later exited the mobile phone manufacturing business taking a charge of just under $1 billion and has since changed its procurement of key components so that, as one manager was quoted as saying in the article, "we will never be exposed like this again."

This story provides perspective on the new world of risk that global organizations face. With the increasing velocity of competition, the unsympathetic nature of markets, and an increasingly "outsourced" world, a seemingly innocuous fire in a supplier's factory in one part of the world dramatically altered the strategic landscape for two organizations in a different industry located in another part of the world.

This example raises a number of management and operational questions about the business designs and organizational processes employed by both companies. However, one question stands out. Was this dramatic shift in Ericsson's strategic position avoidable? And what tools or management processes exist to help managers think about the risk profile created by various operational or business decisions?

---

[1] *The Wall Street Journal*, January 29, 2001, pp. A1, A8.

The Institute of Internal Auditors Research Foundation

Enterprise risk management is one potential solution. It is not clear if either Nokia or Ericsson used an ERM-style approach to understand the risks inherent in the business designs they chose. It is also not clear that ERM could have prevented the business crisis that developed for Ericsson. However, what is clear is that a properly constructed ERM system would have identified this dependence on a single supplier of a critical component potentially driving Ericsson to reassess its supplier arrangements before the fire rather than after the fact.

Defining ERM

Risk management means dealing with uncertainty. ERM is a continuation of a gradual evolution in the risk management landscape (see Figure 0.1).

The term "Enterprise Risk Management" is commonly interchanged with several other terms such as holistic risk management, business risk management, strategic risk management, consolidated risk management, enterprise-wide risk management, or integrated risk management. For the purposes of this report, ERM is defined as:

> "A rigorous and coordinated approach to assessing and responding to all risks that affect the achievement of an organization's strategic and financial objectives. This includes both upside and downside risks."

Why ERM?

Corporate interest in ERM is a function of two key factors:

Regulatory and Oversight Factors

As Table 0.1 shows, since 1994 there is increasing pressure on corporations to improve their governance mechanisms and fully disclose key risk factors and issues. While few of these external groups have recommended ERM explicitly, the nature and scope of their recommendations strongly suggest an ERM-type solution to meet the recommended reporting standards and requirements. However, as this report was being finalized for publication, The Committee of Sponsoring Organizations of the Treadway Commission (COSO) released a Request for Proposal to the marketplace seeking assistance to develop an ERM conceptual framework and application guidance. COSO intends to publish this framework and guidance during the summer of 2002.

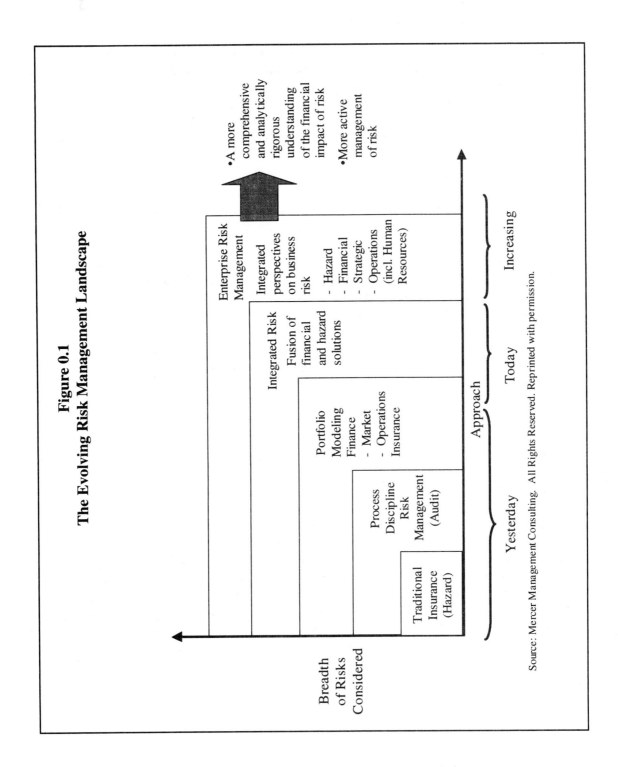

**Figure 0.1
The Evolving Risk Management Landscape**

Source: Mercer Management Consulting. All Rights Reserved. Reprinted with permission.

The Institute of Internal Auditors Research Foundation

Table 0.1: Representative Corporate Governance Initiatives[2]	
Country	**Representative Corporate Governance Initiative(s)**
Canada	■ In Canada, the Dey report, commissioned by the Toronto Stock Exchange and released in December 1994, requires companies to report on the adequacy of internal control. Following that, the clarifying report produced by the Canadian Institute of Chartered Accountants, "Guidance on Control" (CoCo report, November 1995), specifies that internal control should include the process of risk assessment and risk management. While these reports have not forced Canadian listed companies to initiate an ERM process, they do create public pressure and a strong moral obligation to do so. In actuality, many companies have responded by creating ERM processes.
United Kingdom	■ In the United Kingdom, the London Stock Exchange has adopted a set of principles — the Combined Code — that consolidates previous reports on corporate governance by the Cadbury, Greenbury, and Hampel committees. This code, effective for all accounting periods ending on or after December 23, 2000 (and with a lesser requirement for accounting periods ending on or after December 23, 1999), makes directors responsible for establishing a sound system of internal control, reviewing its effectiveness, and reporting their findings to shareholders. This review should cover all controls, including operational and compliance controls and risk management. The Turnbull Committee issued guidelines in September 1999 regarding the reporting requirement for non-financial controls.
Australia and New Zealand	■ Australia and New Zealand have a common set of risk management standards. Their 1995 standards call for a formalized system of risk management and for reporting to the organization's management on the performance of the risk management system. While not binding, these standards create a benchmark for sound management practices that includes an ERM system.

---

[2] Source: Adapted from "Enterprise Risk Management: An Analytic Approach," a Tillinghast-Towers Perrin monograph. Copyright © 2000 Towers Perrin. All Rights Reserved.

Country	Representative Corporate Governance Initiative(s)
Germany	■ In Germany, a mandatory bill — the Kon TraG — became law in 1998. Aimed at giving shareholders more information and control, and increasing the duty of care of the directors, it includes a requirement that the management board establish supervisory systems for risk management and internal revision. In addition, it calls for reporting on these systems to the supervisory board. Further, auditors appointed by the supervisory board must examine implementation of risk management and internal revision.
Netherlands	■ In the Netherlands, the Peters report in 1997 made 40 recommendations on corporate governance, including a recommendation that the management board submit an annual report to the supervisory board on a corporation's objectives, strategy, related risks, and control systems. At present, these recommendations are not mandatory.
United States	■ In the U.S., the SEC requires a statement on opportunities and risks for mergers, divestitures, and acquisitions. It also requires that companies describe distinctive characteristics that may have a material impact on future financial performance within 10-K and 10-Q statements. Several factors broaden the requirement to report on the risks to the organization, leading to setting an enterprise-wide approach to risk management in place: — The report "Internal Control – An Integrated Framework" produced by the Committee of the Sponsoring Organizations of the Treadway Commission (COSO), favors a broad approach to internal control to provide reasonable assurance of the achievement of an entity's objectives. Issued in September 1992, it was amended May 1994. While COSO does not require corporations to report on their process of internal control, it does set out a framework for ERM within an organization.

Country	Representative Corporate Governance Initiative(s)
United States (Cont.)	— In September 1994, the AICPA produced its analysis, "Improving Business Reporting – A Customer Focus" (the Jenkins report), in which it recommends that reporting on opportunities and risks be improved to include discussion of all risks/opportunities that: – Are current. – Are of serious concern. – Have an impact on earnings or cash flow. – Are specific or unique. – Have been identified and considered by management. The report also recommends moving toward consistent international reporting standards, which may include disclosures on risk as is required in other countries. — Institutional investors, such as Calpers, have begun to push for stronger corporate governance and to question companies about their corporate governance procedures — including their management of risk.

Market Factors

Market factors also play an important role in driving organizations to consider ERM. Comprehensive shareholder value management and ERM are inextricably linked. Today's financial markets place substantial premiums for consistently meeting earnings expectations. Not meeting these expectations can result in severe shareholder value punishment in the financial markets. Research conducted by Tillinghast - Towers Perrin (see Figure 0.2 and Appendix III) found that with *all else being equal*, organizations that achieved more consistent earnings than their peers were rewarded with materially higher market valuations.

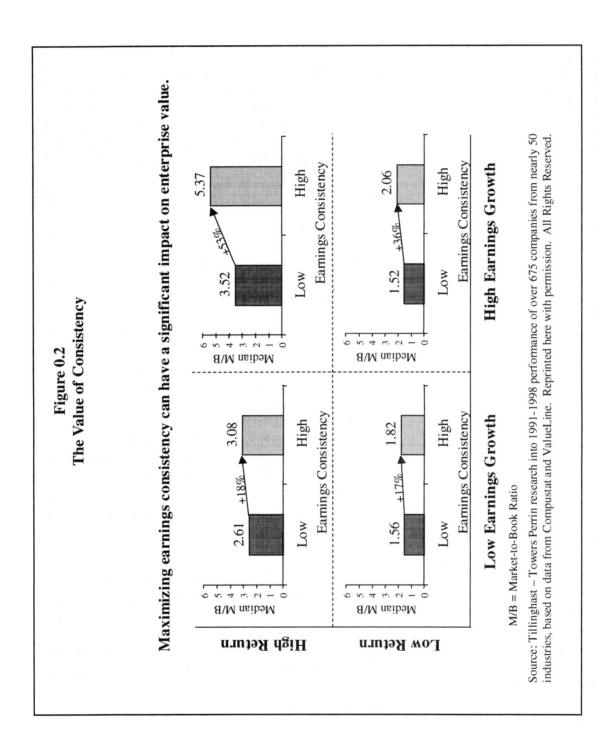

Figure 0.2
The Value of Consistency

Maximizing earnings consistency can have a significant impact on enterprise value.

M/B = Market-to-Book Ratio

Source: Tillinghast – Towers Perrin research into 1991-1998 performance of over 675 companies from nearly 50 industries, based on data from Compustat and ValueLine. Reprinted here with permission. All Rights Reserved.

The Institute of Internal Auditors Research Foundation

Therefore, for corporate executives, managing key risks to earnings is an important element of a shareholder value management agenda. The traditional view of risk management has often focused on property and liability related issues or internal controls. However, as Figure 0.3 demonstrates, "traditional" risk events such as lawsuits and natural disasters may have little or no impact on destroying shareholder value compared to other strategic and operational exposures — such as customer demand shortfall, competitive pressure, and cost overruns. One explanation for this observation is that traditional hazard risks are relatively well understood and managed today — not that they don't matter. Managers now have the opportunity to apply some of the tools and techniques for handling the traditional risks to address all risks that affect the strategic and financial objectives of the organization.

For non-publicly traded organizations, ERM is valuable for many of the same reasons. Rather than from the perspective of shareholder value, ERM would provide managers with a comprehensive overview of other important items such as cash flow risks or stakeholder risks. Regardless of the organizational form, ERM can be an important management tool.

Approaches to ERM

An ERM approach can be viewed in three dimensions (see Figure 0.4). The first represents the range of organization operations. Some organizations have started small by piloting ERM in one, or a small number, of their business units or locations, for real-time fine-tuning and eventual rollout to the entire enterprise. The second dimension represents the sources of risk (hazard, financial, operational, etc.). Other organizations confine the initial scope of ERM to a selected subset of their risk sources, for example, property catastrophe risk and currency risk. Eventually, all sources of risk would be layered in, in sequential fashion.

The third dimension represents the types of risk management activities or processes (risk identification, risk measurement, risk financing, etc.). Some organizations confine their initial vision to the identification and prioritization of enterprise-wide risks, for example, with subsequent activities dependent on the results. Others begin by fashioning an integrated risk-financing program around a subset of risk sources; these often depend on the risk sources for which their financial service providers already have integrated products. Still others begin by measuring and modeling virtually all sources of risk, regardless of their priority and the current availability of risk financing products.

Within this ERM universe, two general models of ERM have emerged: a measurement-driven approach and a process-control approach (see Figure 0.5). We do not believe these are mutually exclusive models. They share many similarities and only differ in their emphasis on certain points — and each carries with it inherent strengths and weaknesses.

The Institute of Internal Auditors Research Foundation

Figure 0.3
Risk Events Causing Large Stock Drops (1993 - 1998)

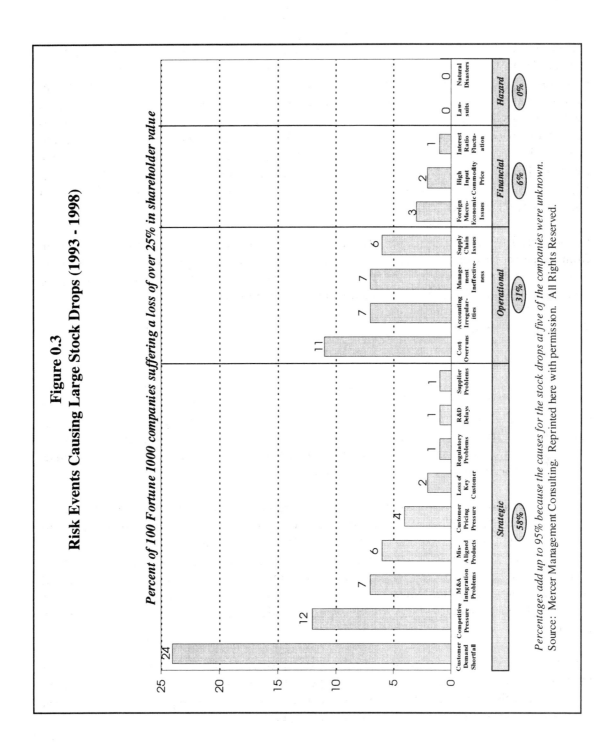

Percent of 100 Fortune 1000 companies suffering a loss of over 25% in shareholder value

Percentages add up to 95% because the causes for the stock drops at five of the companies were unknown.
Source: Mercer Management Consulting. Reprinted here with permission. All Rights Reserved.

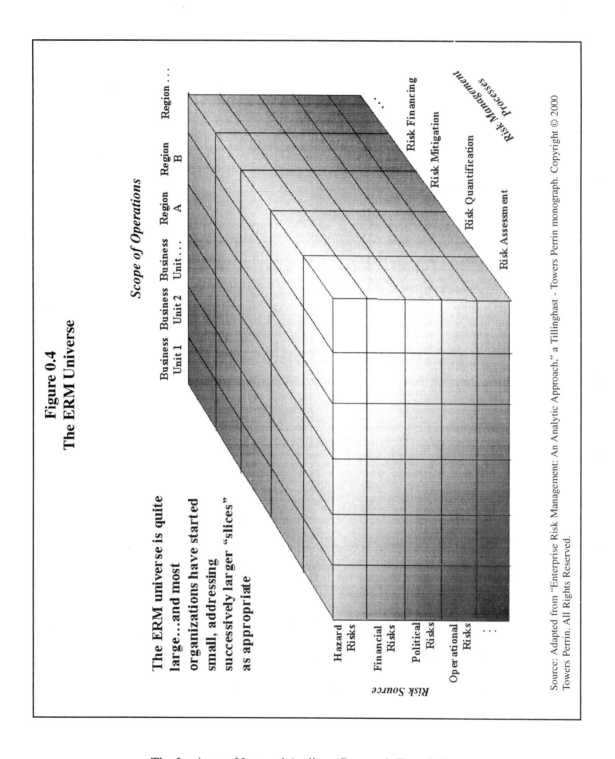

**Figure 0.4
The ERM Universe**

Source: Adapted from "Enterprise Risk Management: An Analytic Approach," a Tillinghast - Towers Perrin monograph. Copyright © 2000 Towers Perrin. All Rights Reserved.

**Figure 0.5
Approaches to ERM**

■ **Measurement-driven approach**: This model focuses on identifying the key risk factors facing an organization and understanding their materiality and probability of occurrence. Risk mitigation activities are focused on the most material risks with appropriate mitigation strategies. (For example, see Figures 0.6 and 0.7)

■ **Process-control approach**: This model focuses on key business processes and accompanying uncertainties in the execution of the business plan. The emphasis is on linking the process steps, reporting relationships, methodologies and data collection and reporting to ensure informed decision-making. The goal is to manage risk events by achieving consistency of application across the business process spectrum thereby limiting the possibility of surprise occurrences. (For example see Figure 0.8)

The Institute of Internal Auditors Research Foundation

In a measurement-driven approach, the focus is on the risks most relevant to the organization (see Figures 0.6 and 0.7). This effectively triages risks and places management attention where it is most needed. One of the possible weaknesses, however, is the risk of a cascading series of events that initially appear small, with a low probability of occurrence and therefore do not make the initial screen, but become significant quickly.

In a process-control approach, the focus is on business processes (see Figure 0.8). This approach does not categorize risks by materiality but rather takes the approach of managing all risks through the consistent, rigorous management of business process steps. Inherent in this model is that good processes can control risks. However, as the Barings collapse emphasized, process controls are only as effective as their application and monitoring.

Each model incorporates the following steps:

- Risk Identification: What are the risks across the various functions and business units in my organization?
- Risk Measurement: What is the relative potential impact of these risk factors?
- Risk Mitigation: What is the best way to manage/eliminate these risks?
- Risk Monitoring: Is my mitigation strategy working?

Unfortunately, there is no single "correct" approach or simple, step-by-step implementation guide to ERM appropriate for all organizations. The correct path is a function of the organization's culture and its unique business circumstances. Although two general approaches have been identified, in practice organizations incorporate elements of both models into their ERM activities. As organizations move forward on ERM, decisions will need to be made on whether a single model of ERM or some adaptation of both models is the most appropriate method.

ERM: A New Tool for Organizational Management?

Using ERM as a management tool has a number of key advantages that organizational leaders should consider. Whether ERM becomes a permanent part of the organizational management lexicon or the latest management fad is still to be determined. While the preceding discussion provided an overview of the issues and approaches to ERM, a number of specific questions remain outstanding about ERM and its role in organizational management:

- What factors are really driving implementation of ERM?
- Is there a relationship between types of industries, size of organization or organizational form and use of ERM?
- Who is responsible for ERM within the organization?

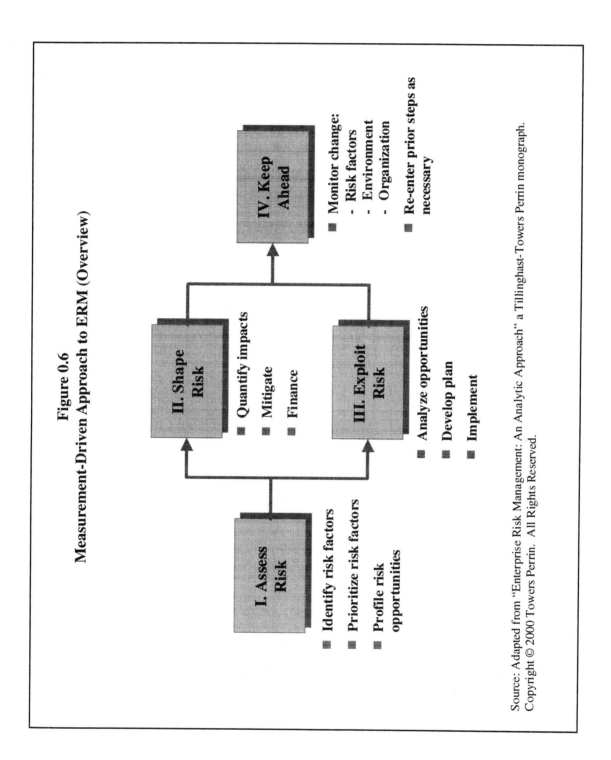

Figure 0.6
Measurement-Driven Approach to ERM (Overview)

Source: Adapted from "Enterprise Risk Management: An Analytic Approach," a Tillinghast-Towers Perrin monograph.
Copyright © 2000 Towers Perrin. All Rights Reserved.

The Institute of Internal Auditors Research Foundation

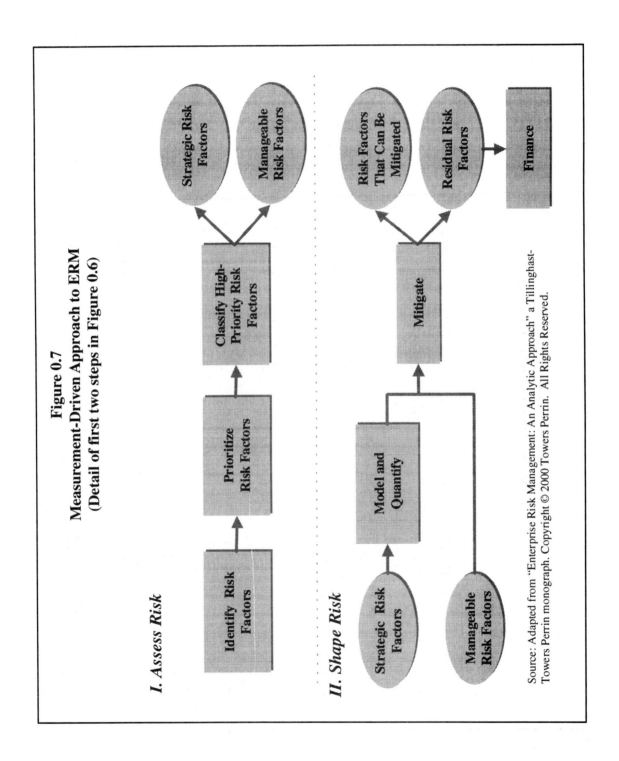

Figure 0.7
Measurement-Driven Approach to ERM
(Detail of first two steps in Figure 0.6)

I. Assess Risk

Identify Risk Factors → Prioritize Risk Factors → Classify High-Priority Risk Factors → Strategic Risk Factors / Manageable Risk Factors

II. Shape Risk

Strategic Risk Factors / Manageable Risk Factors → Model and Quantify → Mitigate → Risk Factors That Can Be Mitigated / Residual Risk Factors → Finance

Figure 0.8
Process-Control Approach to ERM

Examples of Integrated Infrastructure Components -- Sourcing Risk (Procurement) Management

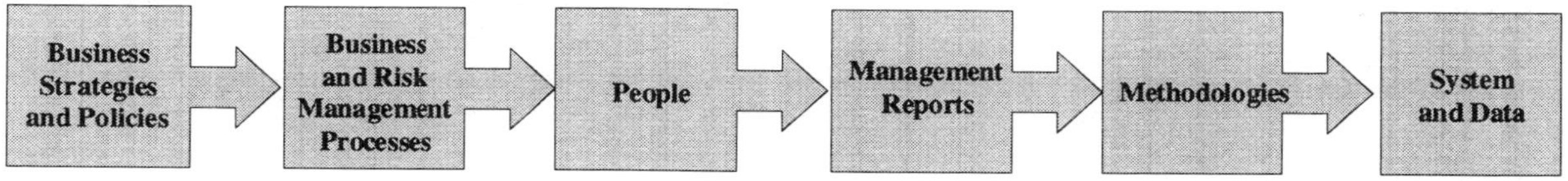

Business Strategies and Policies	Business and Risk Management Processes	People	Management Reports	Methodologies	System and Data
• Supplier strategy	• Supplier certification/ qualification	• Supplier alliances	• Supplier status reports	• Supplier rating system	• Procurement data ware-house
• Supplier selection policy	• Integrated contracting process	• Procurement professionals	• Spending by supplier contract	• Purchasing transaction analysis by contract	• Capture external data
• Ethical standards	• Commodity management	• Cross-functional commodity teams	• Commodity benchmark reports	• Commodity planning	• Procurement system
	• Supplier communications	• Procurement policy committee	• Business process audits	• Commodity benchmarking and intelligence	

Source: Derived from BPRC practice material for inclusion in *Enterprise-wide Risk Management: Strategies For Linking Risk and Opportunity.* Copyright ©2000 Arthur Andersen. All Rights Reserved. Reprinted with Permission.

The Institute of Internal Auditors Research Foundation

- In implementation mode, does ERM truly span the entire organization?
- What types of tools and metrics are being used?

In an attempt to answer these and other questions about the trends and emerging practices in ERM, we conducted a multi-industry global survey. We discuss the major results of the survey in Chapter 1 and provide additional detail and analysis of the survey in Chapter 2.

PART I:
2000 SURVEY OF TRENDS AND EMERGING PRACTICES IN ENTERPRISE RISK MANAGEMENT

The Institute of Internal Auditors Research Foundation

CHAPTER 1
SUMMARY OF MAJOR SURVEY RESULTS

In late 2000, The Institute of Internal Auditors Research Foundation (IIA RF) and Tillinghast-Towers Perrin, in cooperation with The Conference Board of Canada, conducted a multi-industry global survey of chief financial officers, chief audit executives, chief corporate counsels, and chief risk officers to understand trends and emerging practices in ERM.

The survey had over 130 respondents. Over 50 percent of the respondents were publicly held organizations. A number of industries were represented, with the largest single group (approximately 24 percent) being financial services organizations. Energy and mining organizations were the next largest group, comprising approximately 15 percent of the respondents.

Multinational/global organizations (43 percent) were the largest single group of respondents followed by "presence limited to one country" with 19 percent. Organizations with a scope of operations in North America represented 15 percent of respondents. Annual revenue ranged from more than $25 billion (USD) to less than $100 million. Approximately 45 percent of the respondents had between $1 billion and $10 billion in revenues (USD) and nearly 50 percent had between $1 billion and $15 billion in total assets.

A profile of responding organizations is found in Appendix I. Appendix II contains a copy of the survey questionnaire showing complete results.

Summary of Major Survey Results

A desire for a unifying framework and corporate governance regimes are key drivers of ERM

The top five motivating factors driving ERM activity identified were:

- Desire for a unifying framework.
- Corporate governance guidelines.
- Mandate from board of directors.
- Competitive pressure.
- Desire for earnings stability.

More than half of respondents cited the desire for a unifying framework as the primary driver for ERM activity, and 38 percent cited corporate governance guidelines as a key driver.

The Institute of Internal Auditors Research Foundation

Earnings growth and revenue growth are the top business issues today and will continue to be three years from now, and earnings consistency is expected to grow in importance

Participants in the survey were asked to rank order their top business issues today as well as three years from now. Earnings growth received the highest rating in both cases. Similarly, revenue growth was the second highest ranked business issue. Expense control/reduction was ranked as the third most important issue today; however, three years from now earnings consistency was viewed to be the third most important issue.

Organizations view ERM as a tool to help manage their most important business issues

Respondents believe that ERM can help address a number of their top business issues. For each of the top five business issues, more than 55 percent of respondents believe that ERM can help. More than 60 percent of respondents believe ERM can assist with earnings consistency and expense control. Accordingly, while ERM already has some appeal in managing the top business issues, it may have even more significant and immediate value in addressing some of the *underlying* drivers of these issues such as capital management and contingency planning.

ERM tends to be found among larger organizations

Typical profile of respondents with a full or partial ERM framework:

- Publicly held, multinational.
- Revenues and assets in excess of $1 billion (USD).
- ERM framework in place for less than two years.

ERM is still in its earliest stages of application, but few respondents to the survey are ignoring it

The subject of ERM has been a part of the corporate governance discussion for almost a decade. This survey suggests, however, the actual use of ERM as a management and governance tool is a recent phenomenon. For example, approximately 75 percent of organizations using ERM implemented the activity within the last two years.

Moreover, few organizations have implemented a full-scale ERM program. Only 11 percent of survey respondents claimed to have a full ERM system in place. Another 38 percent reported having a partial model. However, 42 percent of survey respondents reported either planning or investigating ERM. This suggests that ERM may be a major point of internal discussion as it relates to corporate governance and value management over the next several years.

Senior executives lead ERM activities, and internal auditing plays a substantial role in implementing ERM

Of the survey respondents, 90 percent noted that risk management and compliance activities are coordinated through a single executive officer. The chief financial officer is the most likely senior executive to oversee risk management or compliance activities.

However, about 30 percent of respondents felt the chief audit executive is or will be responsible for overseeing *enterprise* risk management activities. The CFO was second with 24 percent and the chief risk officer (CRO) was third with 21 percent.

Organizational barriers need to be overcome to implement ERM

Although a large percentage of respondents reported that their organizations are planning or investigating ERM, these organizations are likely to encounter significant organizational barriers in implementing ERM. The top five barriers to implementing ERM for maximum benefit identified by respondents include:

- Organizational culture.
- Benefits are unclear to senior management.
- Lack of formalized process, language, and definitions.
- Organizational "turf."
- Lack of tools.

More than 60 percent of organizations identify implementing risk management programs through a change management model as important. However, only about 20 percent of organizations do it. Also, the low-level use of key levers such as personnel management or compensation as well as the lack of incorporating change processes may make implementation of ERM very difficult. Internal auditing, which may be the implementation arm of an ERM program, should consider the potential importance of these types of linkages.

Comprehensive risk assessments exist in few organizations

Most organizations include financial or operational risks in their internal auditing plan, but less than half consider strategic risks. Moreover, not all organizational functions undergo a formal risk identification and assessment process. For example, 63 percent of respondents reported that the finance function had a formal risk identification and assessment process. In contrast, only 21 percent of respondents reported activity related to the human resource function.

The Institute of Internal Auditors Research Foundation

ERM may initially be more of a management information tool than a driver of corporate performance

There are strong indications from the survey and several of the case studies that some organizations see ERM as an analytical tool rather than as a performance management system at this stage of its development. For example, less than 25 percent of the organizations with full or partial ERM frameworks tie compensation or incentives to their risk management strategies. Additionally, less than a third of all respondents allocate capital or determine capital requirements based on risk measurement.

A variety of tools and metrics are used

Organizations with ERM are more likely than organizations without ERM to employ a wide range of tools ranging from risk mapping to using optimization software. Risk mapping is the most prevalent tool with 50 percent of respondents using it.

The use of other risk metrics is more diffuse. No single metric is used by more than 25 percent of respondents. However, ERM organizations are more likely to use metrics such as Value at Risk and Earnings at Risk than are organizations without ERM. Moreover, fully 30 percent of organizations without ERM report no risk metric is used.

The Institute of Internal Auditors Research Foundation

CHAPTER 2
DETAILED SURVEY RESULTS

Definition of Enterprise Risk Management

For purposes of the survey questionnaire, ERM was defined in the same way as in the Introduction to this report:

A rigorous and coordinated approach to assessing and responding to all risks that affect the achievement of an organization's strategic and financial objectives. This includes both upside and downside risks.

The Current State of ERM

Approximately 50 percent of respondents claimed to have at least a partial ERM framework in place, although just over 10 percent claimed to have a full ERM model (see Figure 2.1). It is important to note that organizations without ERM may have simply declined to participate in this survey. Therefore, the true penetration of ERM may be less than is evident in this survey. Of the organizations with some form of ERM, 75 percent have had it in place less than two years (see Figure 2.2).

Organizations with some form of ERM in this survey were largely publicly held (63 percent) and a majority were multinationals (51 percent) (see Figures 2.3 and 2.4). In terms of revenues, the largest cluster of organizations (37 percent) with ERM fell between $1 billion and $5 billion in revenues (see Figure 2.5). However, just over a quarter of organizations with ERM had less than $500 million in revenue and another 30 percent of organizations had revenue in excess of $5 billion. Viewed another way, 68 percent of organizations with some type of ERM process had in excess of $1 billion in annual revenues.

The financial services industry sector represented the largest single number of organizations with some type of ERM process, representing 27 percent of the total (see Figure 2.6). The energy and mining industry was next with just over 20 percent. Interestingly, public sector organizations rated in the top five industries, ranking ahead of transportation, services, healthcare, retail, or technology industries.

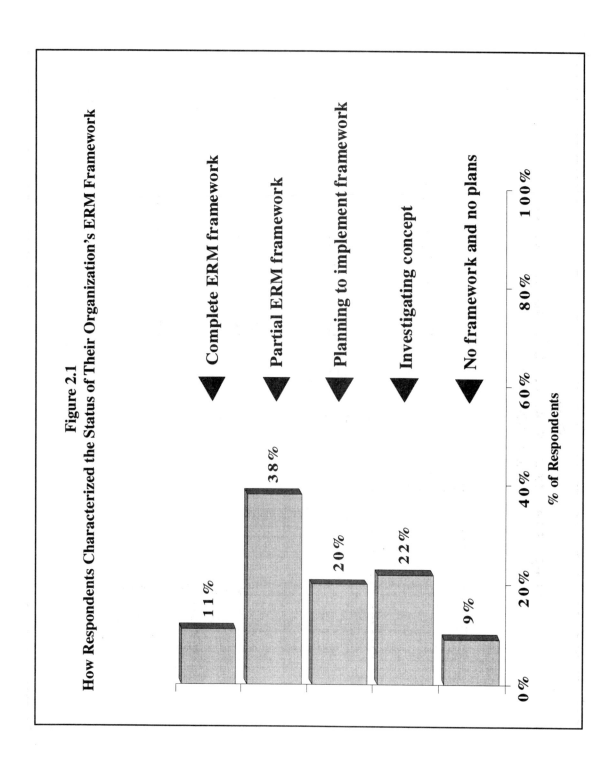

Figure 2.1
How Respondents Characterized the Status of Their Organization's ERM Framework

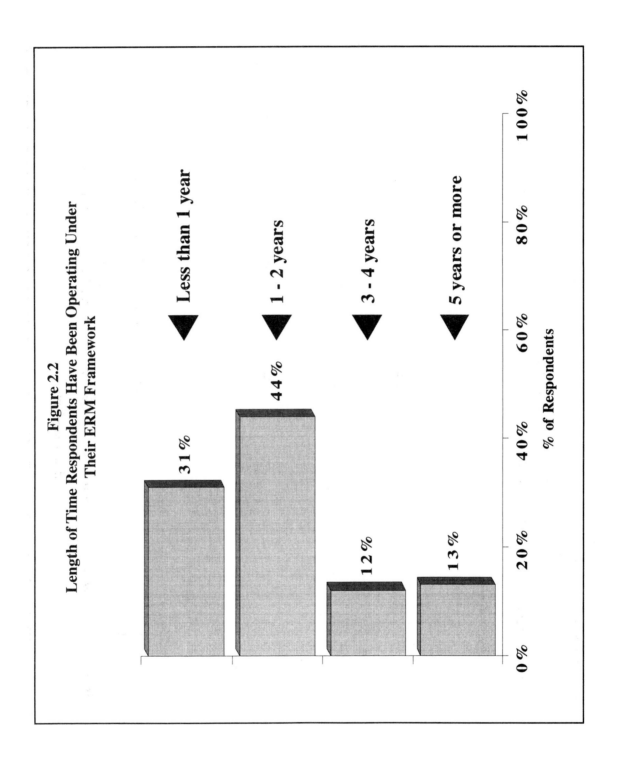

Figure 2.2
Length of Time Respondents Have Been Operating Under
Their ERM Framework

Based on the results of this survey, senior executives are the most likely candidates to oversee an ERM process. For organizations with some form of ERM, 26 percent reported the chief audit executive (CAE) as being responsible for overseeing the ERM process. Chief financial officers and chief risk officers were tied for the next most reported categories at 21 percent of respondents. Less than 10 percent of the organizations reported the CEO and only two percent reported the chief legal officer.

For organizations where ERM is being planned or under consideration, the response was somewhat different. Both the CFO (29 percent) and the CAE (29 percent) were viewed as equally likely to be responsible for the ERM process, but CROs (19 percent) were less likely to manage the ERM process. However, this response may be a function of the current existence of CROs within the respondent organizations. As Figure 2.7 shows, organizations without ERM were less likely to have a CRO. Those non-ERM organizations with CROs are likely banks, at which the CRO may be responsible for market and credit risk, but not other risk categories.

Earlier we identified general pressures driving the implementation of ERM. In this survey, respondents were asked to identify the specific factors motivating their ERM activity. As indicated in Figure 2.8, the desire for a unifying framework for managing risk is by far the most prominent reason for both organizations with an ERM model and for those considering ERM. There is also strong consensus as measured by the similar percentage responses with the role of corporate governance guidelines as a driving factor for ERM. The third most cited driver for those organizations with ERM was the role of a board-level mandate. For those considering ERM, government regulations were the third ranked reason with corporate governance tied with competitive pressures and a desire for earnings stability. The survey results indicated no unique differences based on the geographic scope of the organizations.

These driving pressures become more interesting when viewed in conjunction with the question of barriers to ERM implementation. Figure 2.9 identifies the most significant barriers to implementation. Analysis of the data indicates that organizational issues are among the most important. Organizational culture issues ranked as the top impediment to implementation. "Not perceived as a priority among senior management" was the second top ranked item.

Of the respondents that picked "not perceived as a priority" as the primary impediment to implementing ERM, 69 percent were organizations either planning or investigating ERM. This same group of organizations also cited relatively little influence by boards in driving movement toward ERM in contrast to organizations with some form of ERM. This result suggests that while there are a number of internal and external factors influencing examination of ERM, board-level support may be the key to actually implementing a program.

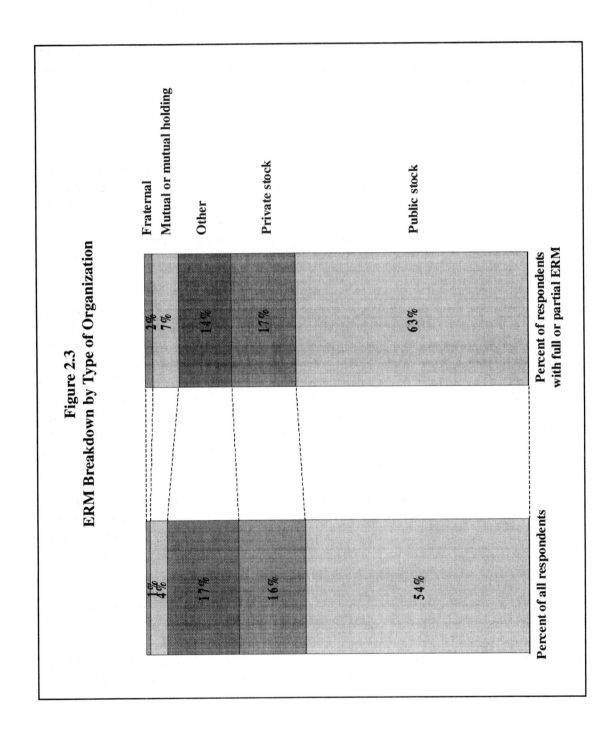

Figure 2.3
ERM Breakdown by Type of Organization

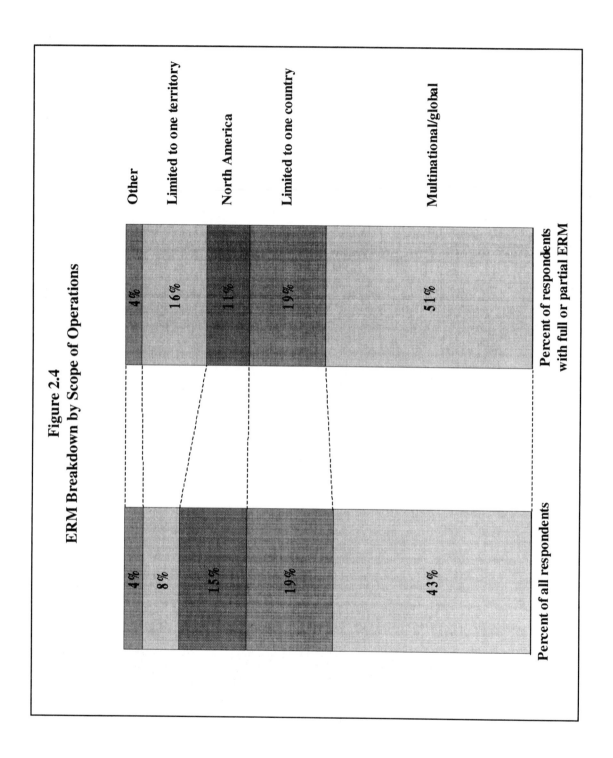

Figure 2.4
ERM Breakdown by Scope of Operations

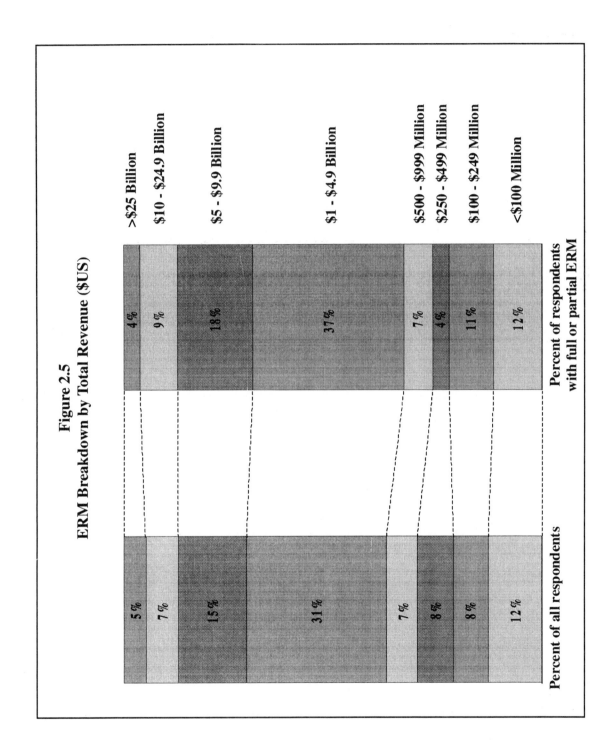

Figure 2.5
ERM Breakdown by Total Revenue ($US)

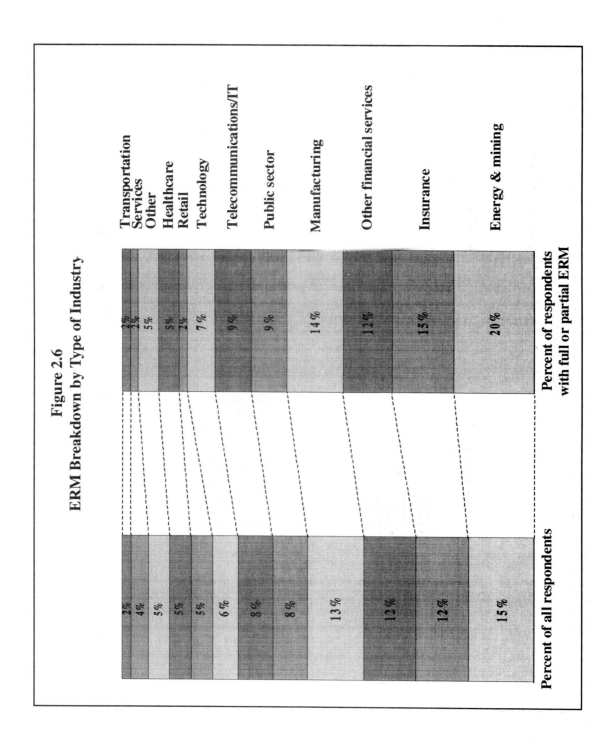

Figure 2.6
ERM Breakdown by Type of Industry

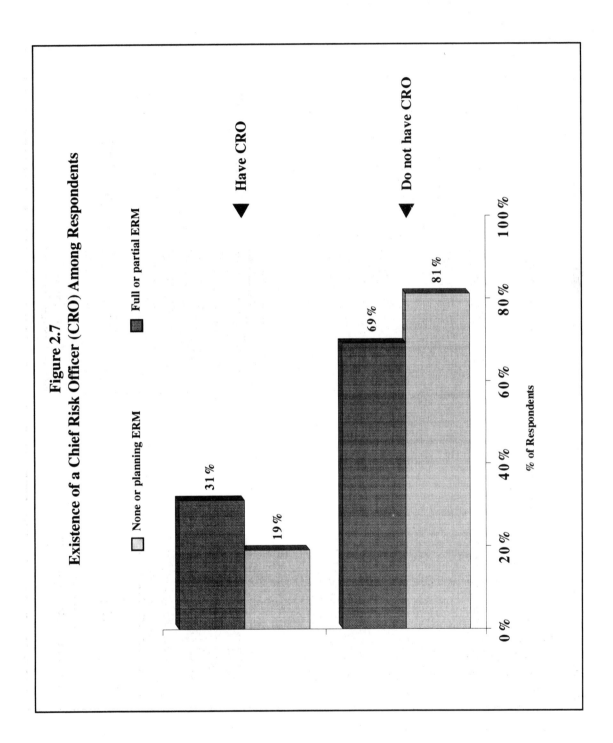

Figure 2.7
Existence of a Chief Risk Officer (CRO) Among Respondents

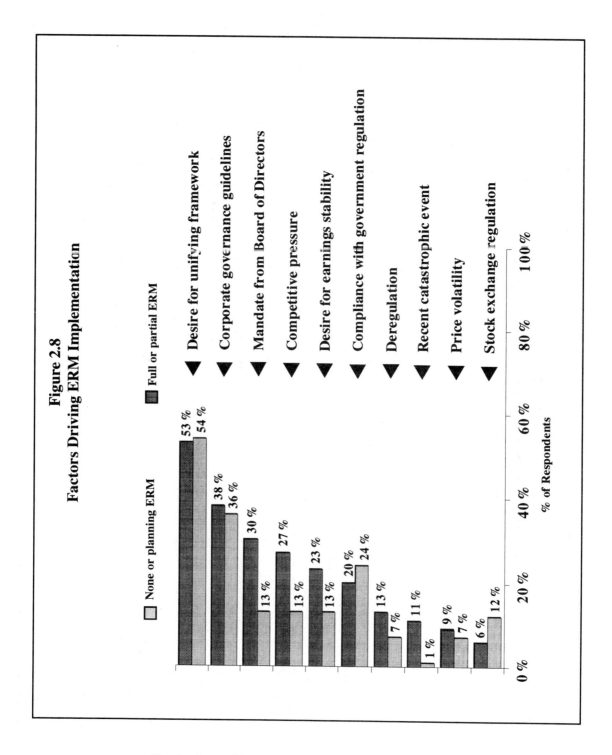

Figure 2.8
Factors Driving ERM Implementation

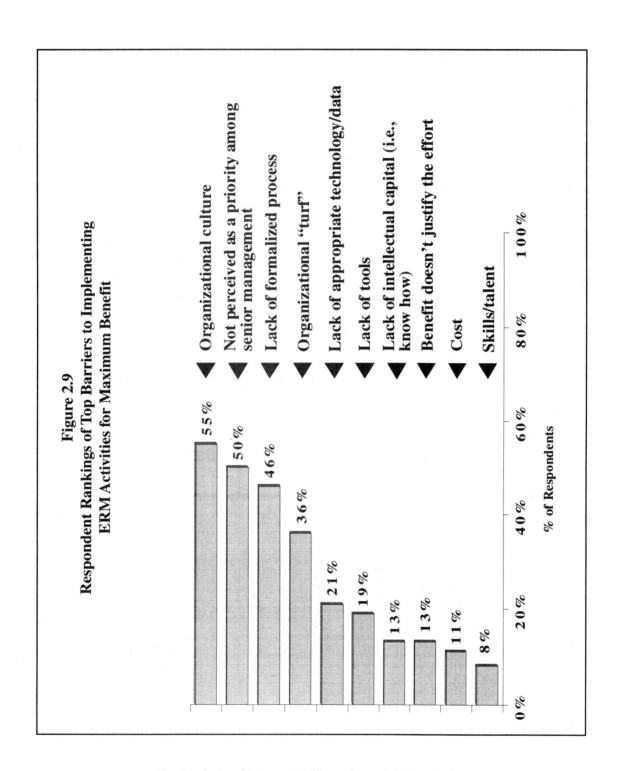

Figure 2.9
Respondent Rankings of Top Barriers to Implementing ERM Activities for Maximum Benefit

Respondents to the survey also noted that lack of a formalized process served as a hindrance to ERM. However, these organizations believed that they possessed the appropriate tools, know how, skills, and technologies to enable ERM. Skills and talent barriers ranked the lowest of all the listed impediments. Lack of intellectual capital ranked the next lowest. As Figure 2.9 demonstrates, lack of technology/data and lack of tools received substantially more votes than any other impediments related to organizational capabilities. However, these two items received almost three times fewer votes than the largest vote total — organizational culture.

Another significant challenge to ERM, although not designated as a barrier in the questionnaire, is the sheer scale and scope of a comprehensive program. As described in the Introduction, ERM is a multidimensional activity with a variety of implementation approaches. Organizations can implement ERM globally and holistically across all risk factors and business units or they can take incremental approaches by focusing on specific risks and/or specific operations and/or specific risk management processes.

Top Business Issues Facing Organizations

Respondents were asked to rank the top five business issues facing their organization from a list of 31, in terms of each issue's importance today and its importance three years from now. Issues were grouped into three categories: general business issues, internal financial/operational issues, and external corporate issues.

Executives say that earnings growth and revenue growth are the top issues now and will still be the top issues three years from now (see Figure 2.10). However, they believe that expense control/reduction will become less important, dropping from the number three to the number six position, and that earnings consistency will become more important, moving from number seven and claiming the number three spot. Additional movements in the top 10 business issues include the dropping of operating controls to the number 13 spot and the movement of capital allocation and management into the top 10 from its 11th spot.

Some interesting comparisons can be drawn between organizations with some form of ERM and those without a current framework. For example, 27 percent of organizations with ERM cited earnings consistency as a top five business issue now. Of these organizations, 34 percent cited it as the top issue three years from now. In contrast only 15 percent of businesses without ERM cited earnings consistency as a top issue today, although 24 percent believe it will be a top issue in three years. On earnings growth as an issue, a similar split occurred. Of the organizations with ERM, 48 percent viewed earnings growth as a top five issue now compared to 34 percent without ERM. Of the ERM organizations that ranked earnings growth as a top five issue now, 50 percent ranked it first. For non-ERM organizations placing earnings growth in the top five, less than 40 percent ranked it first.

Figure 2.10
Top 10 Business Issues Identified by Respondents

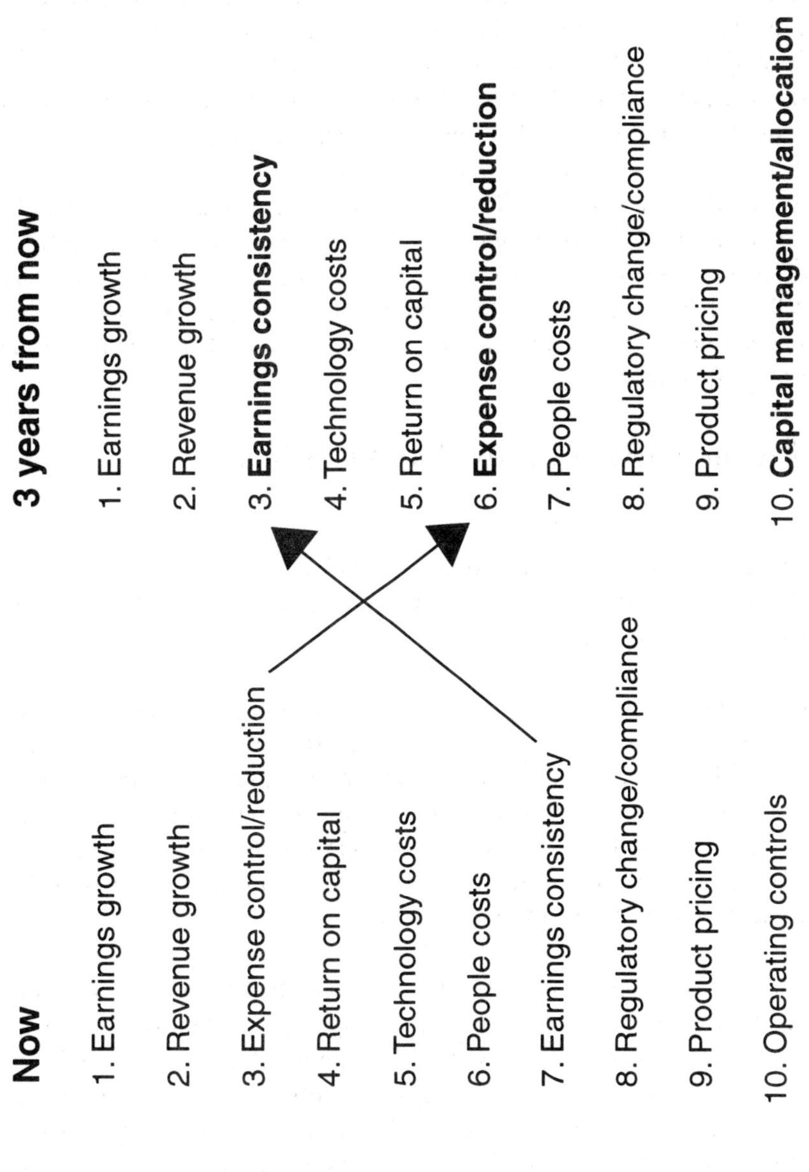

Now

1. Earnings growth

2. Revenue growth

3. Expense control/reduction

4. Return on capital

5. Technology costs

6. People costs

7. Earnings consistency

8. Regulatory change/compliance

9. Product pricing

10. Operating controls

3 years from now

1. Earnings growth

2. Revenue growth

3. **Earnings consistency**

4. Technology costs

5. Return on capital

6. **Expense control/reduction**

7. People costs

8. Regulatory change/compliance

9. Product pricing

10. **Capital management/allocation**

The Institute of Internal Auditors Research Foundation

The majority of respondents believe that ERM will help them address their top 10 issues (see Figure 2.11). In fact, ERM received at least a 50 percent rating across all 31 risk factors.

Closer review of these responses provides some interesting insights into the underlying value and possible evolution of ERM. For example, return on capital is viewed as a top five issue both today and three years from now. While 63 percent of respondents view ERM as helpful with this issue, 85 percent view ERM as helpful with capital management and allocation, a significant driver of return on capital. Additionally, 100 percent of respondents view ERM as helpful with contingency planning and disaster recovery, although these issues did not rank in the top 10. As evidenced in the Nokia/Ericsson situation cited in the Introduction to this report, appropriate contingency planning and disaster recovery programs can play a significant role in helping organizations maintain revenue and earnings growth and consistency.

Risk Management Organization

Risk/Compliance Committees

Respondents to the survey use a variety of managerial and/or board committees to regularly deal with risk management and compliance issues (Figure 2.12). The most widely used committee was the audit committee, cited by 82 percent of organizations. The executive committee played a major role in nearly half of the organizations (47 percent) and a risk management committee was prevalent among 39 percent of respondents. To a lesser degree, the investment committee, asset/liability management committee, and compliance/market conduct committee were also identified as playing a key role in risk management issues, particularly among organizations in the financial services industry.

All of these committees typically include senior management and have broad cross-functional membership. An interesting comparison can be drawn between the key barriers to implementing ERM for maximum benefit (e.g., organizational culture, lack of formalized processes) and the fact that these committees are composed of senior management who clearly seem to be in a position to deal with these barriers.

A small number of survey respondents cited other committees that are involved in risk management, including:

- Credit.
- Environmental.
- Operations.
- Strategic planning.

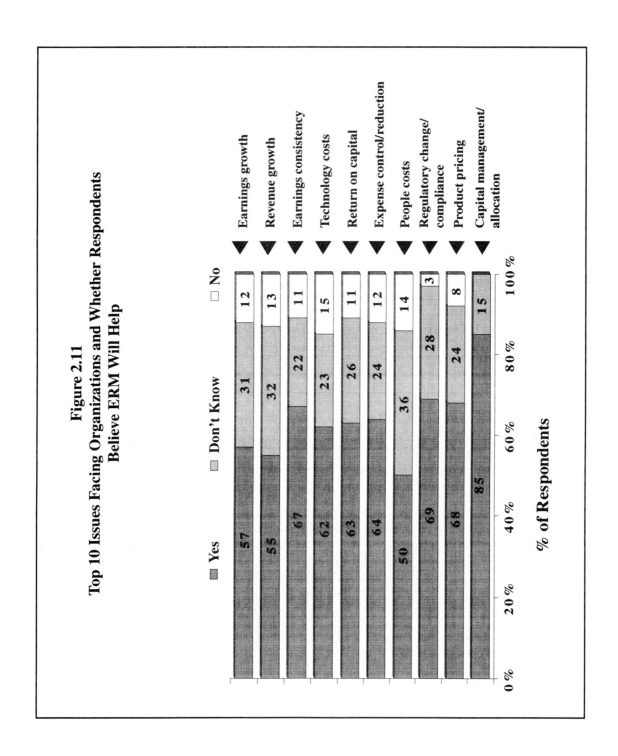

Figure 2.11
Top 10 Issues Facing Organizations and Whether Respondents
Believe ERM Will Help

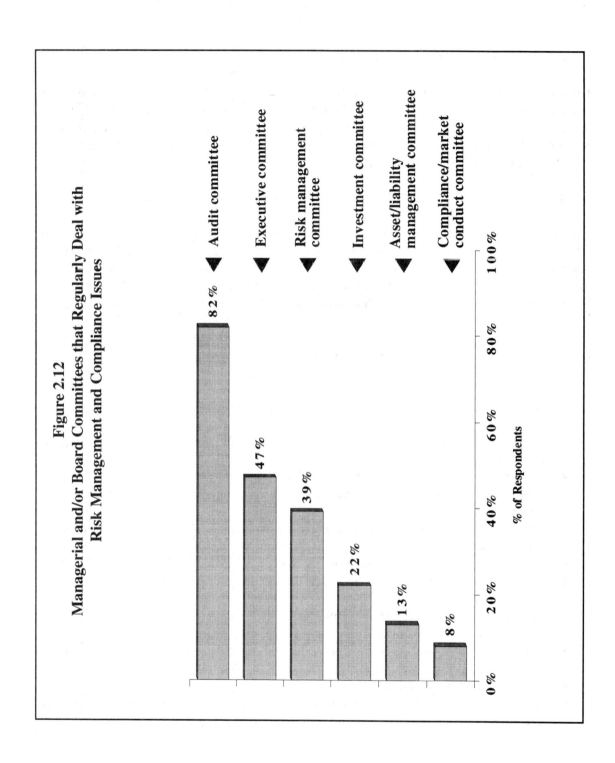

Figure 2.12
Managerial and/or Board Committees that Regularly Deal with Risk Management and Compliance Issues

Coordination/Integration of Activities

Organizations coordinate their various risk management committees and activities in a number of ways (see Figure 2.13). A vast majority of these committees report to a single executive officer — in most instances, the CFO or CEO. At some organizations, either the CRO or CAE takes the lead in coordinating these committees/activities. At just over 20 percent of the organizations, these activities are guided by a board mandate.

Internal Auditing

In many organizations, the internal auditing function plays a role in assessing and responding to risks that affect the organization. Nearly 90 percent of the respondents reported that internal auditing conducts risk-based audits at the business unit level. About one-third said that internal auditing participates to some extent on ERM committees or working teams. Approximately one-third of the respondents also indicated that internal auditing conducts ERM risk assessments (see Figure 2.14).

Respondents identified a number of other ways in which internal auditing can or should play a role in risk management, including:

- Greater coordination with other risk management activities in the organization to prioritize risk assessment activities.
- Auditing compliance with financial risk management policies, legal actions/statutes, and regulations.
- Getting more involved in new ventures and mergers and acquisitions.
- Letter of representation from business units which states the risks and mitigation tactics for each business unit.
- Should be directly involved in the governance process and ethical conduct expectations and compliance.
- Actively participate on technology project steering committees.
- Assist with the assessment process and determine adequacy of controls once in place.
- ERM system analysis.
- Reporting risk profiles to the CEO, top executives and the board.
- Operational risk management.
- Stimulating discussion, debate, and awareness among senior management and the board around the topic of risk management.
- Risk management committee.
- Helping to keep the risk model current. Aggregating risk among business units to a corporate-wide exposure. Updating the audit committee on the success of the program.

The Institute of Internal Auditors Research Foundation

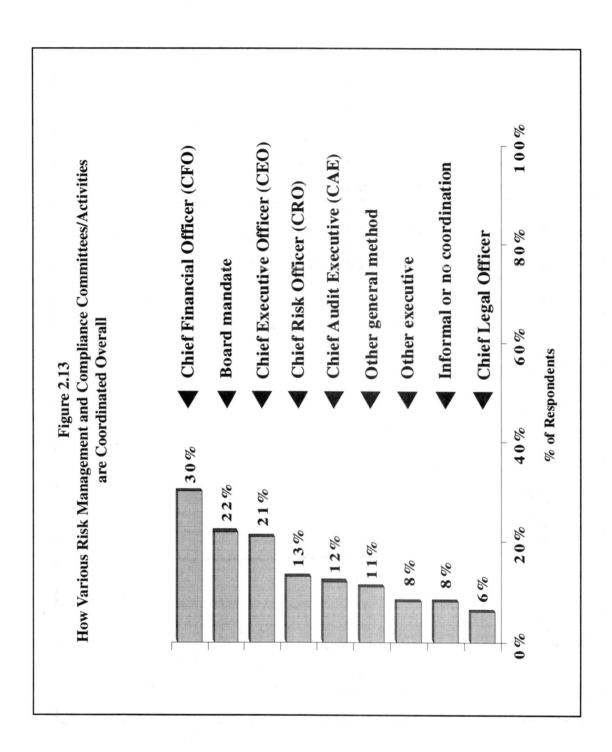

Figure 2.13
How Various Risk Management and Compliance Committees/Activities are Coordinated Overall

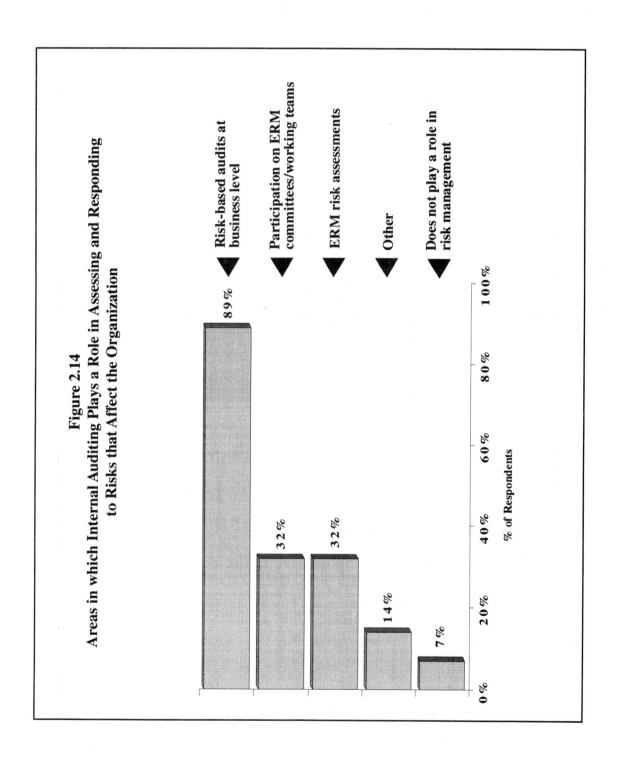

Figure 2.14
Areas in which Internal Auditing Plays a Role in Assessing and Responding
to Risks that Affect the Organization

- Possible involvement in risk management from insurance perspective.
- Internal auditing should conduct workshops to help minimize risk in all areas.
- Consolidating the risk assessment results into an auditing plan.
- Developing the ERM framework, methodology, and common risk language.
- Monitoring of implemented risk mitigation strategies for compliance with previous recommendations.
- Credit risk management, financial risk management, business continuity planning, and information technology security.

Chief Risk Officer. Nearly a quarter of the organizations (24 percent) reported having a CRO. This is consistent with the results from two recent surveys by Tillinghast - Towers Perrin of executives from financial services organizations. The organizations that have this position reported that it is fairly new — over 90 percent said it was established within the past four years and just over 60 percent indicated that the CRO position has been in place for two years or less (see Figure 2.15).

This position typically reports to the CEO, CFO, or in some fashion to the board of directors (see Figure 2.16). For organizations with ERM, CROs are more likely to report to the CEO (43 percent) than non-ERM organizations (25 percent). Over 70 percent of the organizations with a CRO said that the person filling that position came from an internal source — primarily from either an internal auditing or finance function, with 10 percent coming from the risk management function (see Figure 2.17). A variety of functions from throughout the organization report to the CRO.

Risk Sources, Treatment, Procedures and Tools

Based on the results of the survey, internal auditing plans cover a wide spectrum of risk areas. Figure 2.18 shows the types of risks covered by auditing plans and their corresponding percentages.

As the figure shows, nearly every organization surveyed audits financial risk issues. However, less than half the respondents include strategic risks in their auditing plans. Firms with some type of ERM process are a bit more likely to include strategic risks in their internal auditing programs. Of the organizations with some type of ERM process, 54 percent incorporate strategic risks, whereas only 43 percent of organizations without an ERM program include strategic risk factors in their internal auditing plans.

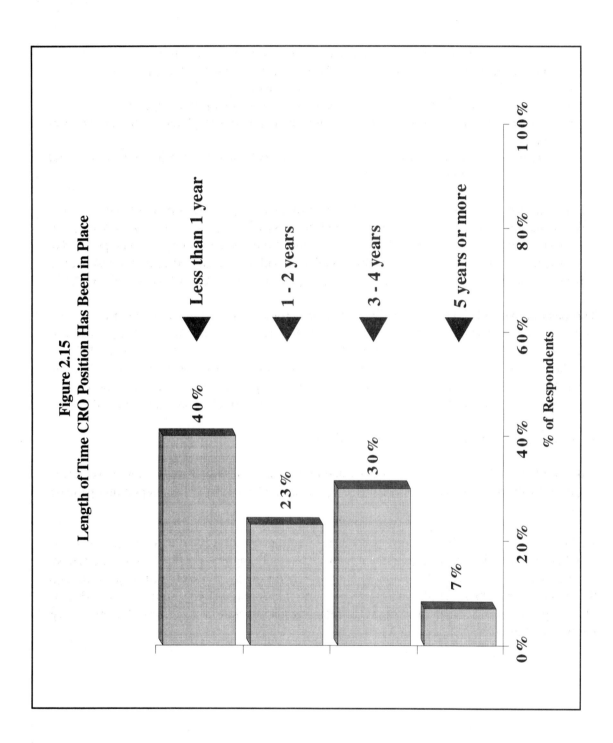

Figure 2.15
Length of Time CRO Position Has Been in Place

The Institute of Internal Auditors Research Foundation

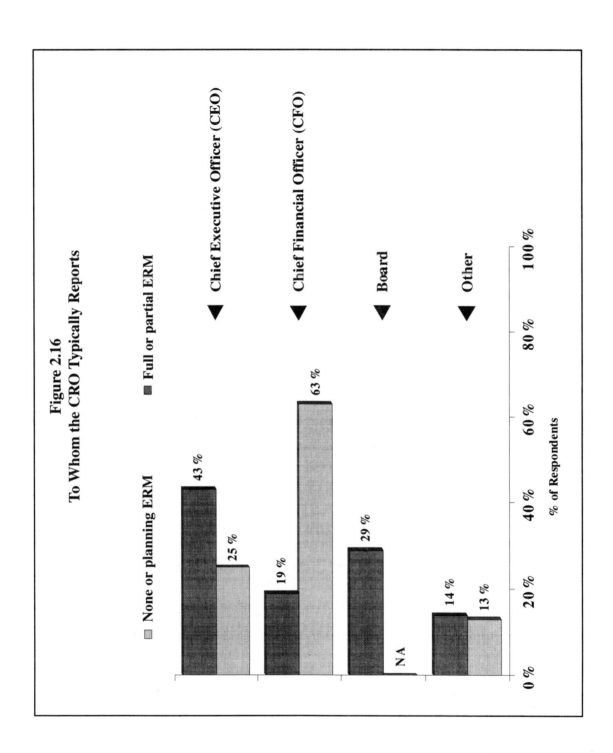

Figure 2.16
To Whom the CRO Typically Reports

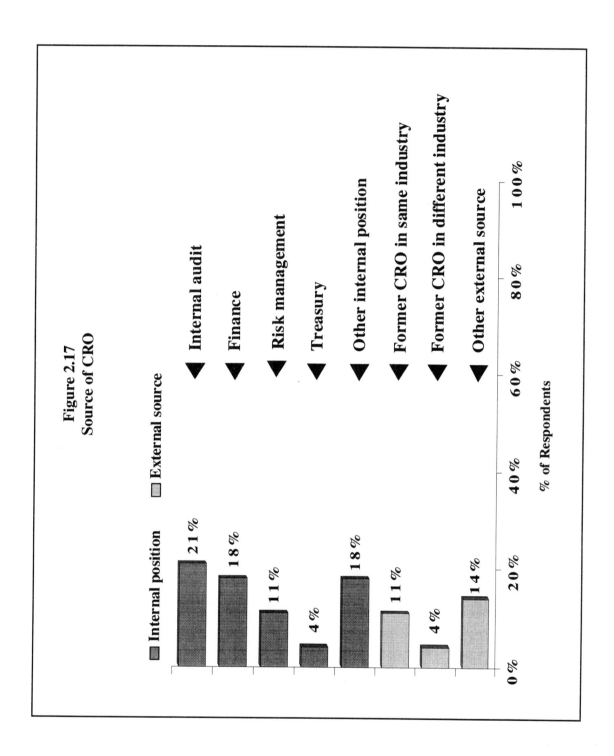

Figure 2.17
Source of CRO

The Institute of Internal Auditors Research Foundation

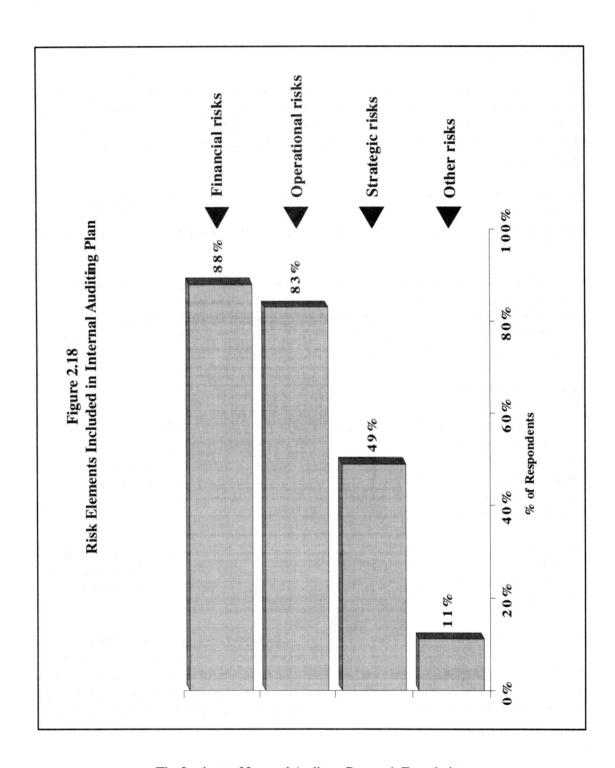

Figure 2.18
Risk Elements Included in Internal Auditing Plan

Risk Sources

We asked respondents to rate the importance of a number of different risk sources and tell us whether they are actively managing that risk source (see Figure 2.19). Executives assigned the highest importance ratings to five risk sources (using a weighted average score based on a five-point scale). A complete list of the risk sources and their relative weighted average scores are available in Appendix II.

With the exception of reputation/rating, each of the top five risk factors fell into the operational risk category. There was also complete consensus that each of these five risk sources will have some form of program in place over the next three years to manage any exposures the organization may have to them.

What is interesting to note is the high ranking of people and intellectual capital. It is tied as the most important risk source with reputation/rating. However, among the top five issues only two-thirds of organizations actively manage people/intellectual capital risks. In contrast, approximately 75 percent of organizations manage the next three issues with the number five issue, expense control, receiving the highest level of management (80 percent).

Risk Assessment

Based on the results of the survey, each of the top five risk sources will likely have some form of active management in place within the next three years. Human resource and intellectual capital issues may require significant more effort to put in place risk measurement systems. Only 21 percent of organizations surveyed had formal risk identification and assessment processes in place for human resources, the lowest percentage of all the functions. However, when responses are analyzed based on their ERM status, significant differences emerge.

For example, 31 percent of organizations with some form of ERM program have specific risk assessment and identification programs for human resources. In contrast, only 12 percent of organizations without an ERM program evaluated risk factors in the human resource field (see Figure 2.20).

As expected, organizations with some form of ERM are more likely to have formal risk identification and assessment processes across other functions than those organizations without an ERM model. However, despite an ERM framework, several functions in addition to human resources are less likely to receive a formal review. Less than 50 percent of procurement, legal, and sales and marketing functions within the respondent organizations receive any form of formal risk identifi-

The Institute of Internal Auditors Research Foundation

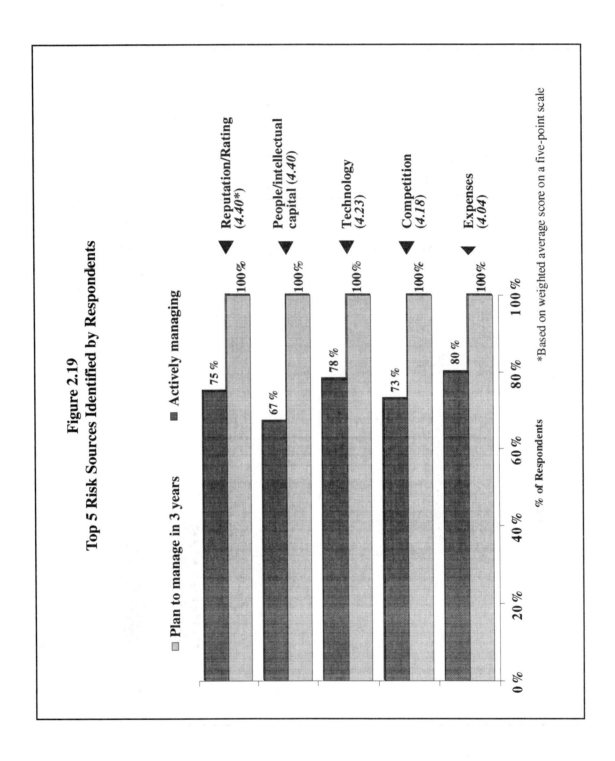

Figure 2.19
Top 5 Risk Sources Identified by Respondents

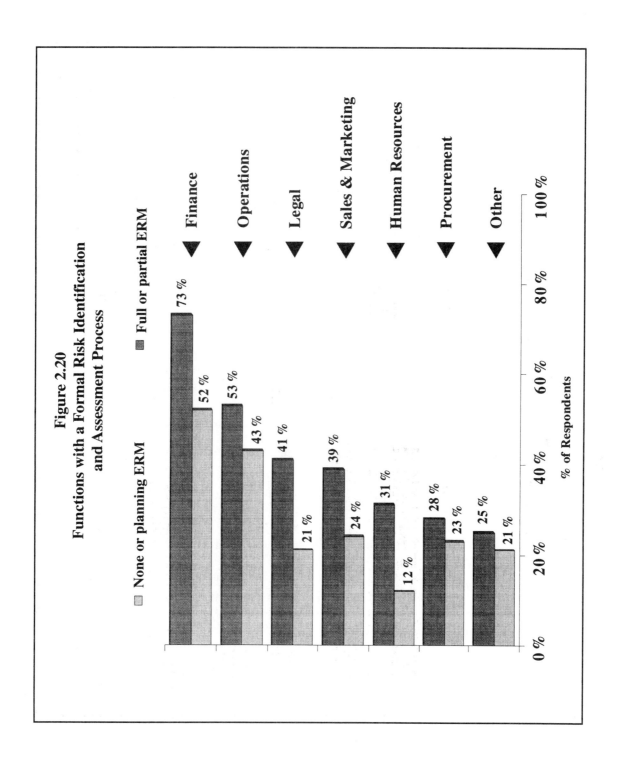

Figure 2.20
Functions with a Formal Risk Identification and Assessment Process

None or planning ERM   Full or partial ERM

Finance

Operations

Legal

Sales & Marketing

Human Resources

Procurement

Other

73 %
52 %
53 %
43 %
41 %
21 %
39 %
24 %
31 %
12 %
28 %
23 %
25 %
21 %

0 %   20 %   40 %   60 %   80 %   100 %

% of Respondents

cation and assessment process. More than half (56 percent) of the organizations have one or two functions that undergo some form of formal risk identification and assessment process (see Figure 2.21). Only 25 percent of organizations have five or more functions that undergo this type of review.

Risk Management Procedures

Organizations were asked to provide inputs on 18 key risk management procedures. They were asked three questions:

- Whether they consider the procedure important.
- Whether they use the procedure.
- If not used, whether they planned to implement it within the next three years.

The responses for each risk management procedure are summarized in Figures 2.22 through 2.39. Each figure represents one risk management procedure and they are placed in order according to their importance ranking among total respondents. We also provide a breakdown for each procedure relative to its importance and use by ERM status. We also identify the size of the gap between the importance and use rankings for each procedure. We determined the size of the gaps by simply subtracting a procedure's current usage level from its perceived importance.

Analysis of the data suggests a tiering based on perceived importance according to the following:

- Top tier: importance rankings greater than 70% (see Figures 2.22 through 2.27).
- Second tier: importance rankings between mid-60% to 70% (see Figures 2.28 through 2.31).
- Third tier: importance rankings between mid-50% and mid-60% (see Figures 2.32 through 2.35).
- Fourth tier: importance rankings of 50% and below (see Figures 2.36 through 2.39).

The most important procedure, identified by 86 percent of respondents, was the ranking of risk factors based on their materiality (see Figure 2.22). The next two highest ranked procedures, conducting formal enterprise-wide risk assessments and using a coherent framework to guide risk activities, were tied at 82 percent (see Figures 2.23 and 2.24).

The high level of importance attributed to these top tier procedures also translated into implementation. The most important procedures also ranked among the highest in use. This pattern generally held true among all the responses. Risk management procedures in the top tier were used on

Figure 2.21
Number of Functions that Have Formal Risk Identification
and Assessment Process

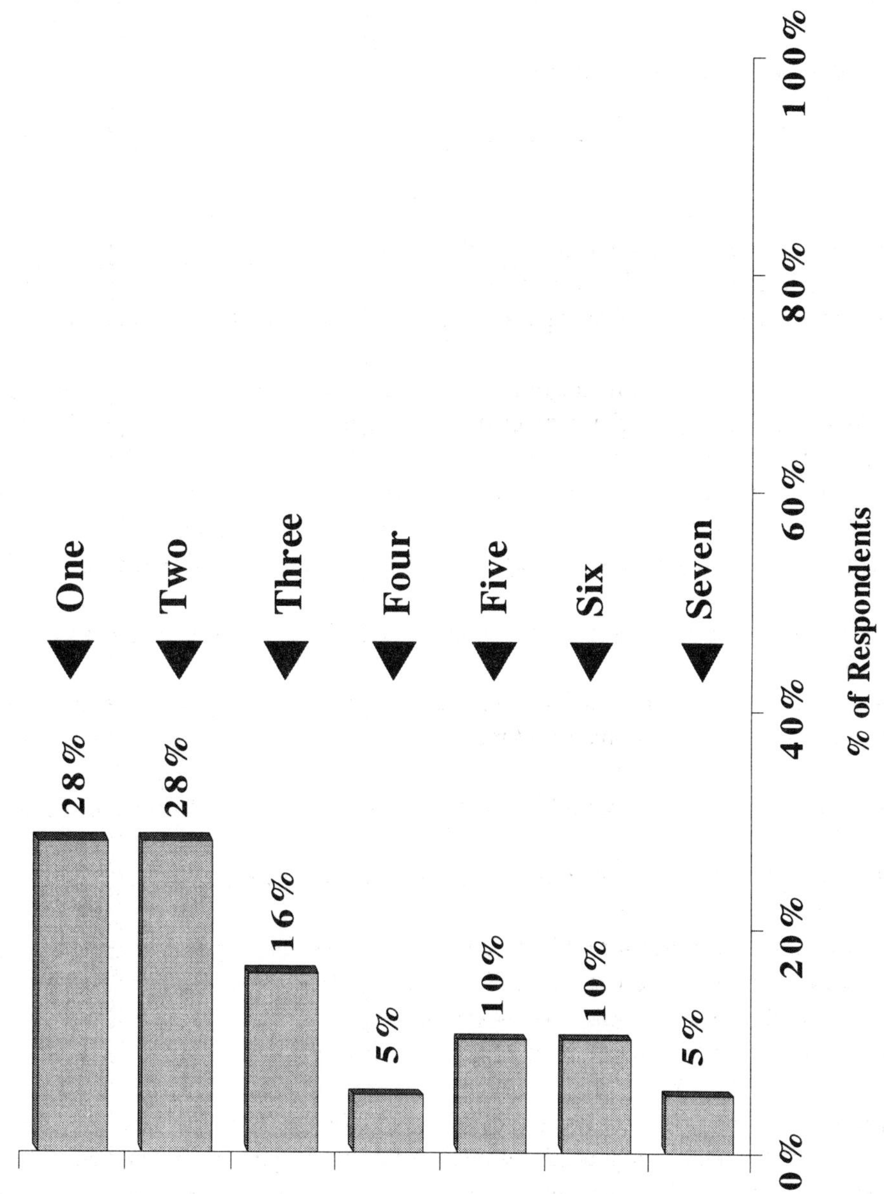

% of Respondents

The Institute of Internal Auditors Research Foundation

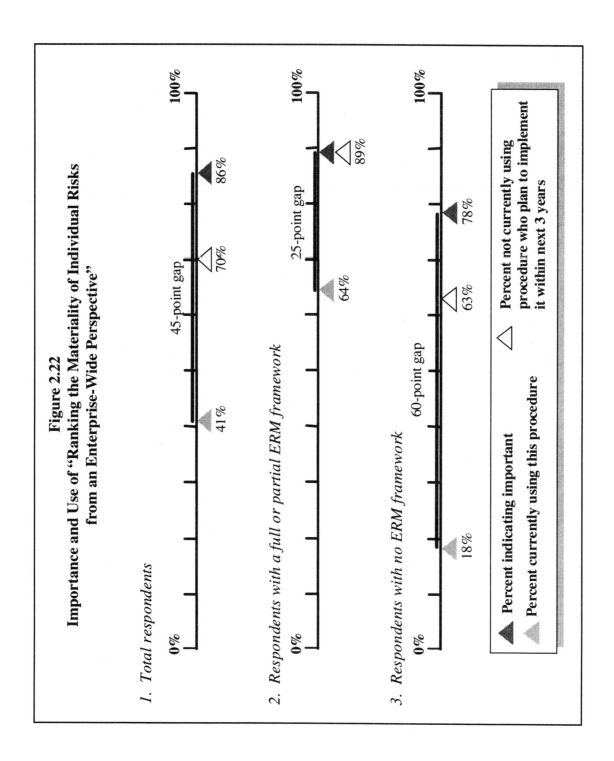

Figure 2.22

Importance and Use of "Ranking the Materiality of Individual Risks from an Enterprise-Wide Perspective"

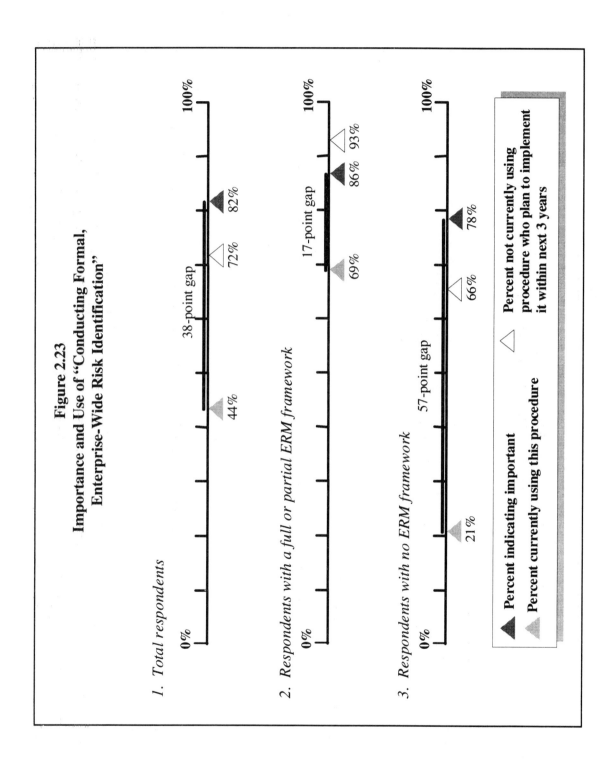

Figure 2.23
Importance and Use of "Conducting Formal,
Enterprise-Wide Risk Identification"

1. Total respondents

0%   100%

38-point gap

44%   72%   82%

2. Respondents with a full or partial ERM framework

0%   100%

17-point gap

69%   86% 93%

3. Respondents with no ERM framework

0%   100%

57-point gap

21%   66%   78%

◀ **Percent indicating important**   △ **Percent not currently using**
                                          procedure who plan to implement
◀ **Percent currently using this procedure**   **it within next 3 years**

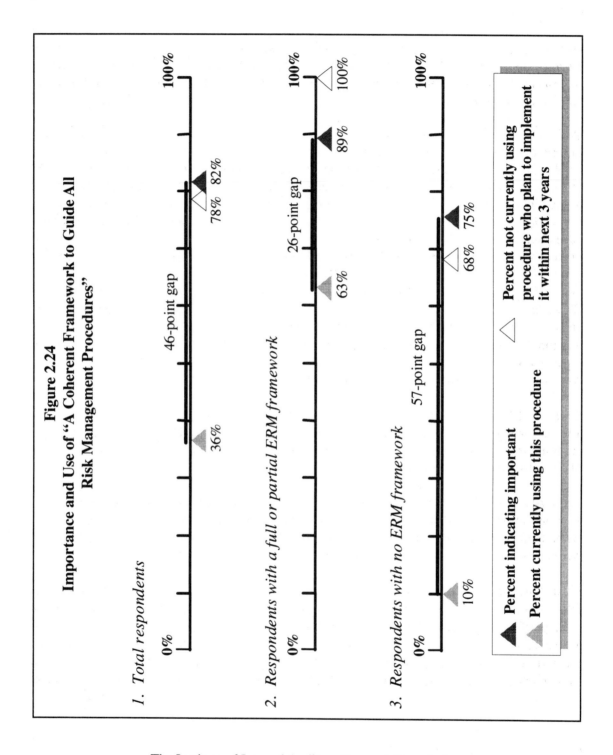

Figure 2.24
Importance and Use of "A Coherent Framework to Guide All
Risk Management Procedures"

1. *Total respondents*

0% 46-point gap 100%
36% 78% 82%

2. *Respondents with a full or partial ERM framework*

0% 26-point gap 100%
63% 89% 100%

3. *Respondents with no ERM framework*

0% 57-point gap 100%
10% 68% 75%

▲ **Percent indicating important**
△ **Percent not currently using procedure who plan to implement it within next 3 years**
▲ **Percent currently using this procedure**

average by approximately 40 percent of respondents whereas organizations used the procedures in the lower tiers less than 25 percent on average. One important exception was the use of integrated risk financing products where 36 percent of respondents reported using this method despite its relatively low level of recognition (55 percent) as an important procedure (see Figure 2.25).

The next highest ranked group of procedures clustered around return on capital issues. The highest ranked procedure in this group (67 percent of respondents identified this procedure as important) involved the measurement of risk management strategies relative to the risk/return requirements of the business. However, only 24 percent of organizations actually use this procedure. This is one of the highest importance/use gaps in the survey. All of the other procedures related to return on capital have importance/use gaps of at least 35 points. Unlike the procedures in the top tiers which have future implementation rates in excess of 70 percent, future implementation of the second tier procedures are between approximately 40 percent and 50 percent (see Figures 2.28 through 2.31).

Several of the third tier procedures raise some important questions regarding implementation of ERM. For example, 63 percent indicated that incorporating risk management into personnel management or executive compensation programs is important. However, only 15 percent actually use that model — the biggest importance/use gap in the survey. Moreover, less than 40 percent of organizations not linking risk to personnel management or executive compensation are likely to do so within the next three years (see Figure 2.32).

Similarly, 60 percent of respondents identified implementing risk management programs through a formal change approach as important. Only 21 percent of organizations actually use a change program and only 35 percent of those organizations not currently using a change program are likely to use one going forward (see Figure 2.33).

These procedures have particular resonance based on other survey results. Seventy-three percent of organizations stated that they would implement some type of ERM program within three years. As noted earlier in this report, organizational issues related to culture, turf, and perceived priority were identified as some of the significant barriers to implementation of ERM.

Finally, the fourth tier represents a mix of procedures (see Figures 2.36 through 2.39). They range from tools to measure risks to mechanisms to transfer risks. Only 41 percent of organizations rated using portfolio enhancement techniques as important — the lowest score in this part of the survey. Moreover, only 18 percent of organizations use this technique and only 22 percent of those not presently using it plan to do so within the next three years. Securitizing risks also received a similar low score. Only 45 percent of organizations viewed this as important and only 26 percent

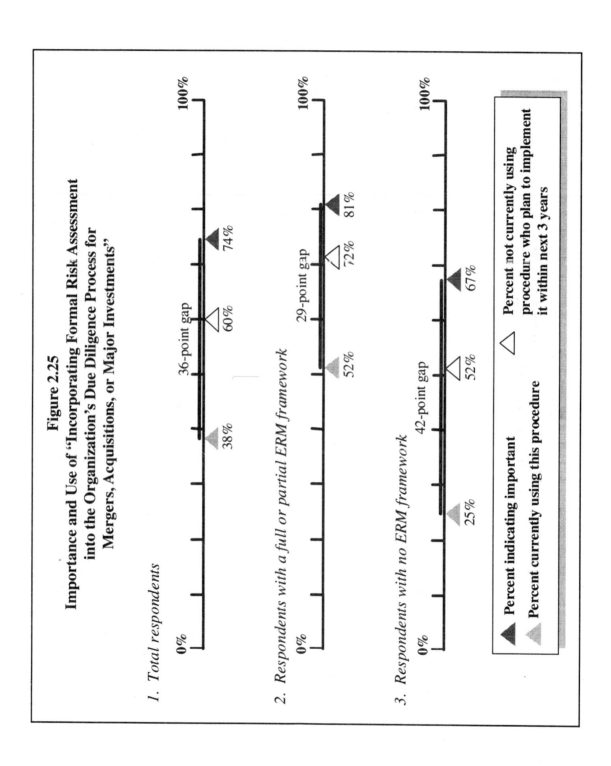

Figure 2.25
Importance and Use of "Incorporating Formal Risk Assessment into the Organization's Due Diligence Process for Mergers, Acquisitions, or Major Investments"

1. Total respondents

2. Respondents with a full or partial ERM framework

3. Respondents with no ERM framework

◀ Percent not currently using procedure who plan to implement it within next 3 years

◁ Percent indicating important

◀ Percent currently using this procedure

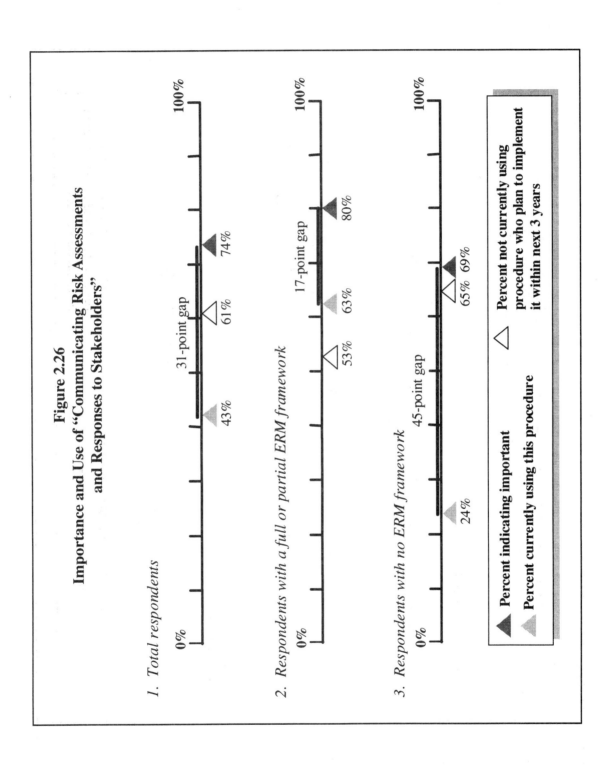

Figure 2.26
Importance and Use of "Communicating Risk Assessments
and Responses to Stakeholders"

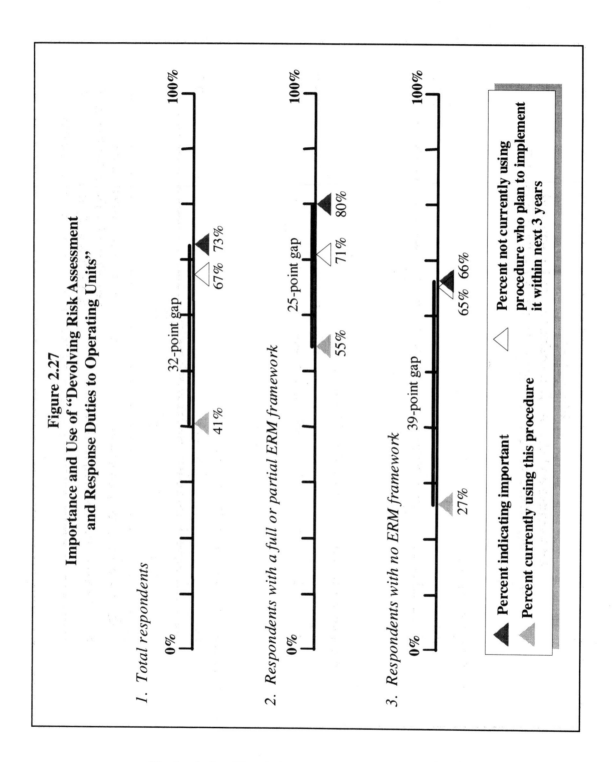

Figure 2.27
Importance and Use of "Devolving Risk Assessment and Response Duties to Operating Units"

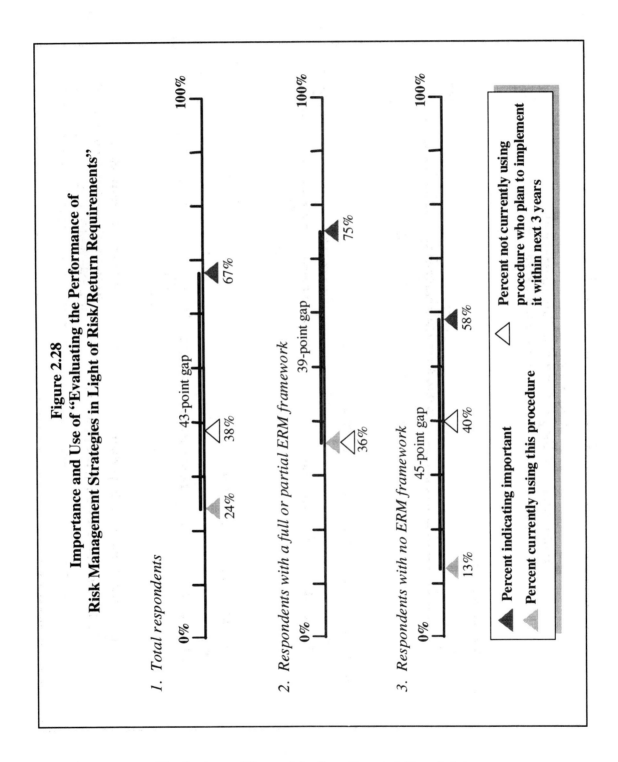

Figure 2.28
Importance and Use of "Evaluating the Performance of
Risk Management Strategies in Light of Risk/Return Requirements"

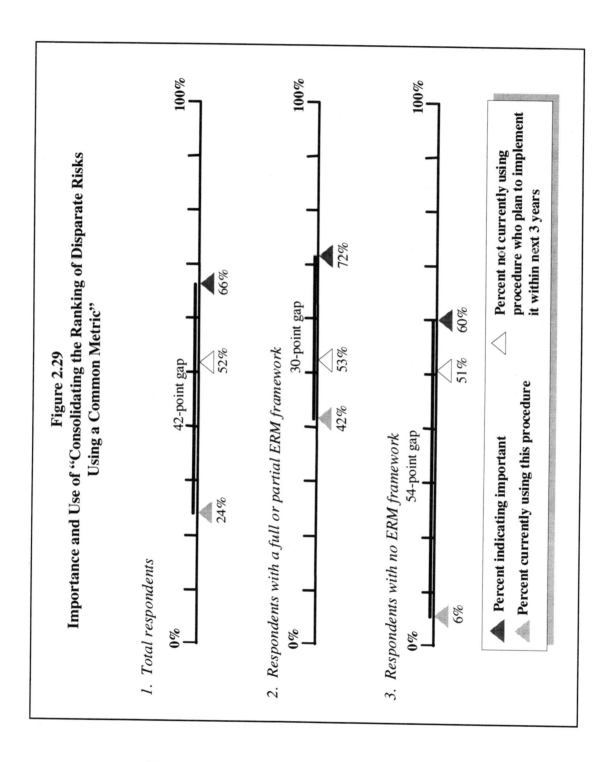

Figure 2.29

Importance and Use of "Consolidating the Ranking of Disparate Risks Using a Common Metric"

1. *Total respondents*

0% — 24% — 42-point gap — 52% — 66% — 100%

2. *Respondents with a full or partial ERM framework*

0% — 42% — 30-point gap — 53% — 72% — 100%

3. *Respondents with no ERM framework*

0% — 6% — 54-point gap — 51% — 60% — 100%

▲ **Percent indicating important**
▲ **Percent currently using this procedure**

△ **Percent not currently using procedure who plan to implement it within next 3 years**

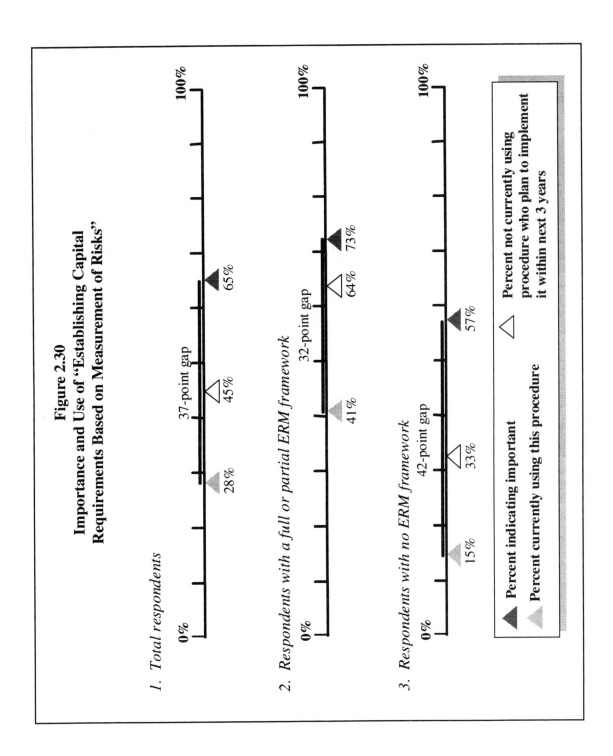

Figure 2.30
Importance and Use of "Establishing Capital
Requirements Based on Measurement of Risks"

1. Total respondents

0%   37-point gap   100%
                  45%   65%
         28%

2. Respondents with a full or partial ERM framework

0%   32-point gap   100%
                  64%   73%
              41%

3. Respondents with no ERM framework

0%   42-point gap   100%
                  33%   57%
         15%

▲ **Percent indicating important**   △ **Percent not currently using**
                                         procedure who plan to implement
                                         it within next 3 years

◣ **Percent currently using this procedure**

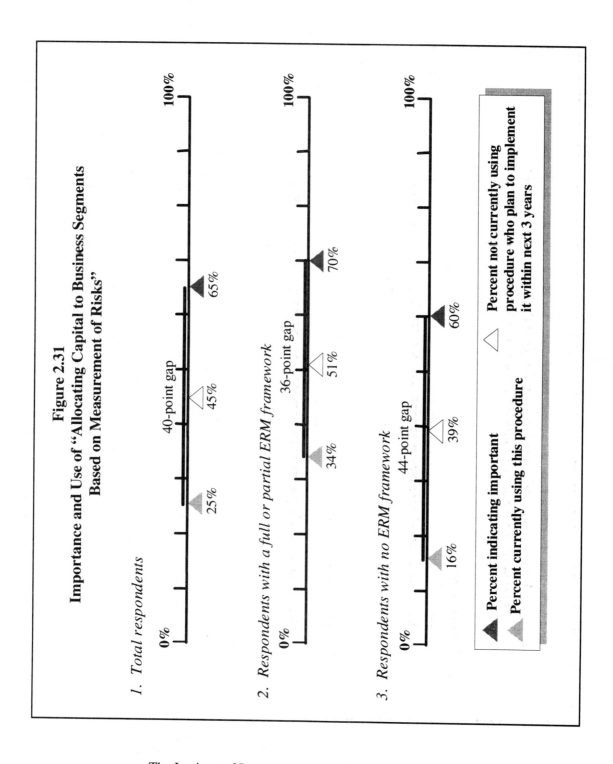

Figure 2.31
Importance and Use of "Allocating Capital to Business Segments Based on Measurement of Risks"

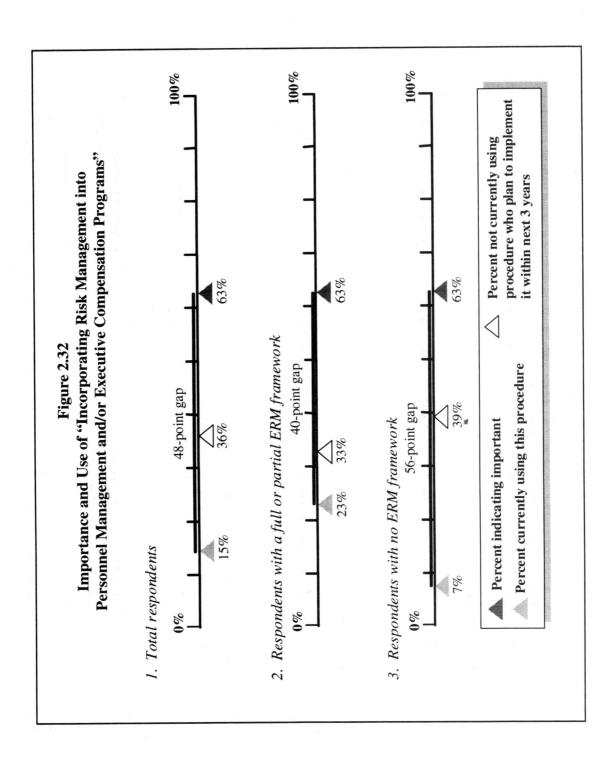

Figure 2.32

Importance and Use of "Incorporating Risk Management into Personnel Management and/or Executive Compensation Programs"

1. Total respondents

2. Respondents with a full or partial ERM framework

3. Respondents with no ERM framework

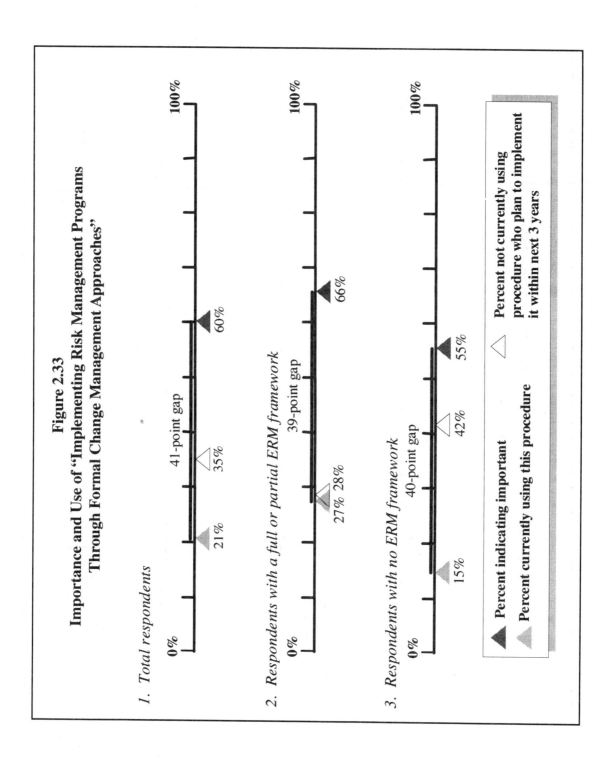

Figure 2.33
Importance and Use of "Implementing Risk Management Programs Through Formal Change Management Approaches"

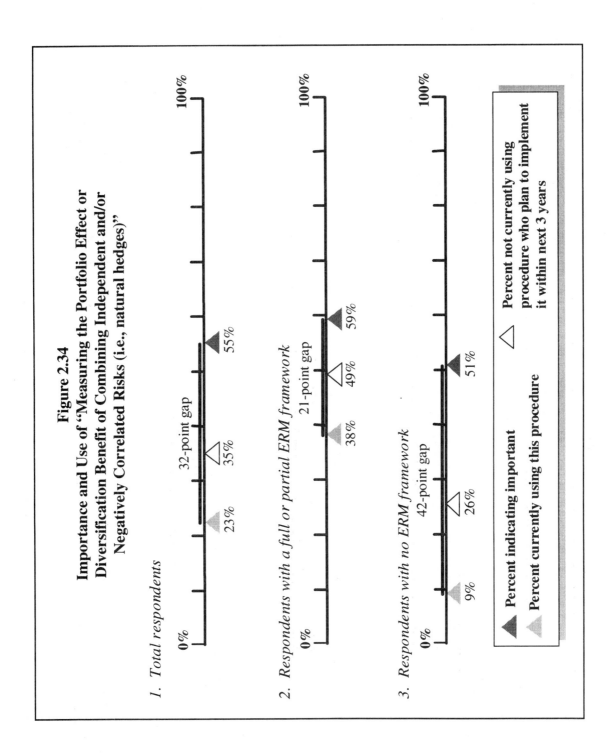

Figure 2.34

Importance and Use of "Measuring the Portfolio Effect or Diversification Benefit of Combining Independent and/or Negatively Correlated Risks (i.e., natural hedges)"

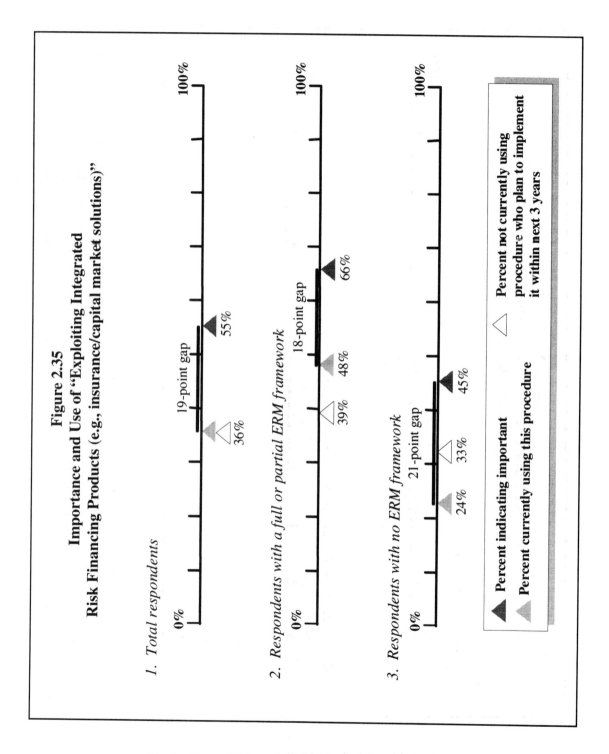

Figure 2.35
Importance and Use of "Exploiting Integrated
Risk Financing Products (e.g., insurance/capital market solutions)"

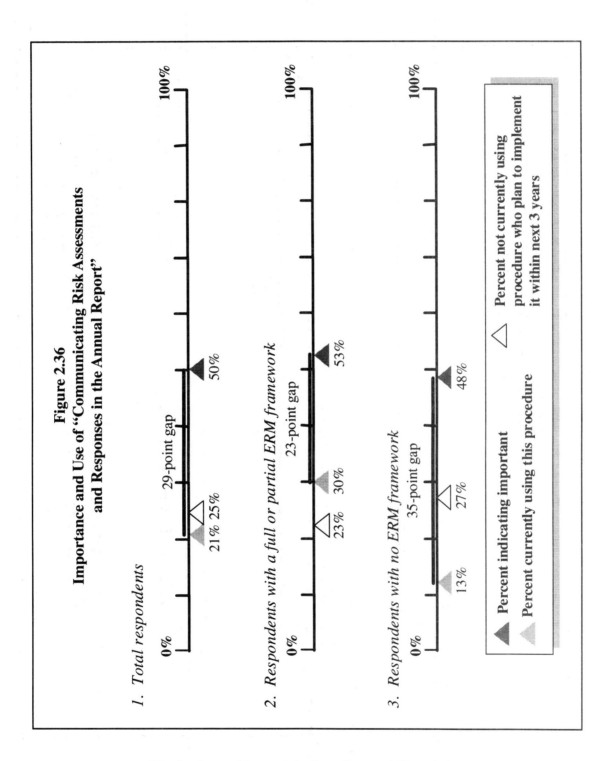

Figure 2.36

Importance and Use of "Communicating Risk Assessments and Responses in the Annual Report"

1. Total respondents

29-point gap

21% 25%   50%

2. Respondents with a full or partial ERM framework

23-point gap

23%   30%   53%

3. Respondents with no ERM framework

35-point gap

13%   27%   48%

◀ Percent indicating important

◀ Percent currently using this procedure

◁ Percent not currently using procedure who plan to implement it within next 3 years

The Institute of Internal Auditors Research Foundation

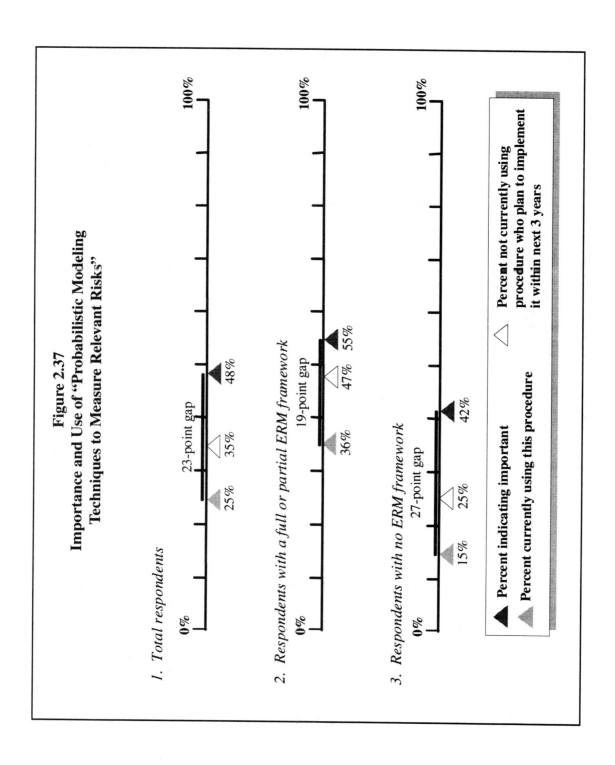

Figure 2.37
Importance and Use of "Probabilistic Modeling Techniques to Measure Relevant Risks"

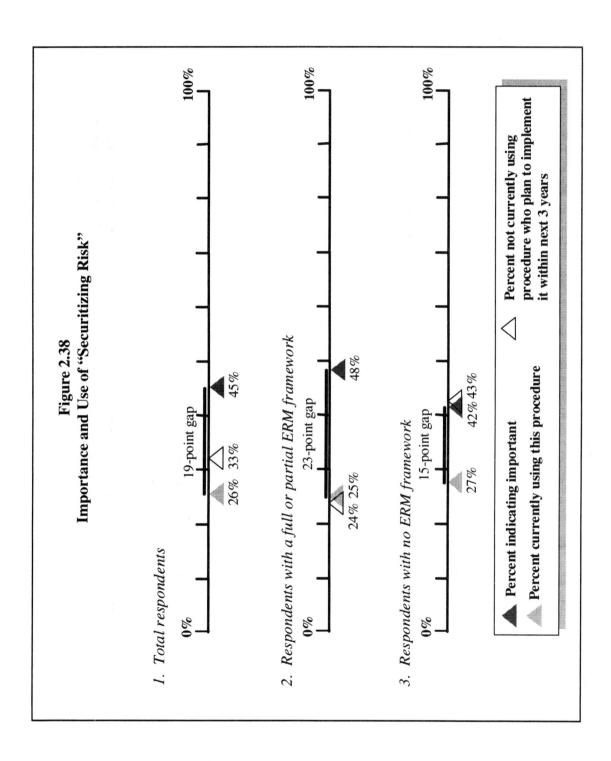

Figure 2.38
Importance and Use of "Securitizing Risk"

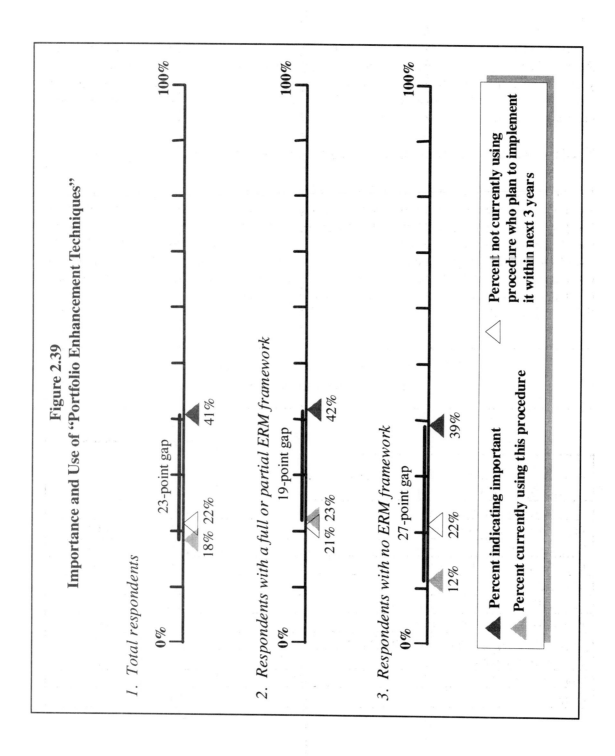

Figure 2.39
Importance and Use of "Portfolio Enhancement Techniques"

1. *Total respondents*

23-point gap

0%   18% 22%   41%   100%

2. *Respondents with a full or partial ERM framework*

19-point gap

0%   21% 23%   42%   100%

3. *Respondents with no ERM framework*

27-point gap

0%   12%   22%   39%   100%

▲ **Percent indicating important**
△ **Percent not currently using procedure who plan to implement it within next 3 years**
▲ **Percent currently using this procedure**

of respondents use risk securitization — one of the lowest importance/use gaps in the survey. Another 33 percent of those not using this tool today were likely to use it within the next three years. Finally, just fewer than 50 percent of organizations viewed probabilistic modeling techniques to measure risks as important. Only 25 percent actually use it and only 35 percent of non-users are likely to use it going forward.

Tools Used to Implement Risk Management Procedures

Use of sophisticated modeling tools does not have much penetration among the organizations surveyed. As Table 2.1 shows, statistically based modeling tools are used as a primary tool among less than 30 percent of total respondents. Simulation tools as a primary technique are used in less than 15 percent of organizations. However, for organizations that employ some type of ERM, the use of these tools is higher than for organizations without some type of ERM program. Of the organizations with ERM, 30 percent use a simulation technique such as Monte Carlo or a stochastic model, whereas less than 20 percent of organizations without ERM use some form of simulation (see Table 2.2).

Table 2.1: Types of Tools Used to Implement Risk Management Procedures		
Type of Tool	**Primary Tool(s)**	**Secondary Tool(s)**
Risk mapping of individual risks (e.g., using frequency/ severity maps)	50%	9%
Risk assessment workshops	44%	9%
Pro forma financial modeling	28%	13%
Scenario planning	20%	19%
Management "dashboards"	15%	6%
Monte Carlo simulations	14%	11%
Probabilistic (stochastic) simulation	11%	13%
Economic scenario generation	10%	18%
Behavior modification performance incentives	9%	10%
Catastrophe modeling	8%	14%
Optimization software	4%	8%
Other	3%	2%

The Institute of Internal Auditors Research Foundation

Moreover, in organizations with some type of ERM program, activities such as risk assessment workshops are nearly twice as likely to occur than in organizations without ERM (see Table 2.2). "Management dashboards" are also twice as likely to occur. It is interesting to note that organizations without ERM programs are more likely to employ behavior modification incentives (22 percent versus 16 percent for organizations with ERM).

Clearly organizations with some form of ERM are more likely to use a range of tools compared to those without ERM. However, linking ERM to behavior change programs through the incentive or personnel performance management system has not had any greater penetration in ERM organizations than in non-ERM organizations. This suggests that today ERM is viewed more as a management information device and not yet as a driver of corporate performance.

Table 2.2: Types of Tools Used to Implement Risk Management Procedures by ERM Status		
Type of Tool (either primary or secondary)	**Full or Partial ERM**	**None or Planning ERM**
Risk mapping of individual risks (e.g., using frequency/ severity maps)	75%	43%
Risk assessment workshops	70%	37%
Pro forma financial modeling	44%	39%
Scenario planning	41%	37%
Economic scenario generation	31%	24%
Monte Carlo simulations	30%	19%
Probabilistic (stochastic) simulation	30%	18%
Management "dashboards"	28%	13%
Catastrophe modeling	20%	24%
Behavior Modification Incentives	16%	22%
Optimization software	14%	9%

Metrics Used to Measure ERM Activities

Table 2.3 identifies the metrics used by organizations. To measure ERM activities, the top primary metric used is Value at Risk (VAR). It is also the top overall metric used by 33 percent of organizations. Table 2.4 shows the types of metrics used by ERM status. VAR is the top ranked metric regardless of ERM status. However, 42 percent of organizations with some form of ERM use it compared to only 24 percent without an ERM program.

Table 2.3: Types of Metrics in Place		
Type of Metric	**Primary Metric(s)**	**Secondary Metric(s)**
Value at Risk (VAR)	22%	11%
Cost of Risk (COR)	21%	3%
Return on Capital Employed (ROC or ROCE)	18%	6%
Mark-to-Market	17%	5%
Risk Adjusted Return on Capital (RAROC)	12%	8%
Economic Value Added™ (EVA)	12%	8%
Earnings at Risk	11%	10%
Probability of Ruin	7%	4%
Expected Cost of Ruin	5%	4%
Mark-to-Future™	2%	2%
Below Target Risk	1%	5%
Other	5%	NA
No metric currently being used	24%	NA

The Institute of Internal Auditors Research Foundation

Table 2.4: Types of Metrics in Place by ERM Status		
Type of Metric (either primary or secondary)	**Full or Partial ERM**	**None or Planning ERM**
Value at Risk (VAR)	42%	24%
Cost of Risk (COR)	33%	15%
Earnings at Risk	33%	9%
Mark-to-Market	27%	16%
Risk Adjusted Return on Capital (RAROC)	25%	16%
Return on Capital Employed (ROC or ROCE)	23%	24%
Economic Value Added™ (EVA)	22%	19%
Probability of Ruin	14%	7%
Expected Cost of Ruin	11%	6%
Mark-to-Future™	6%	1%
Below Target Risk	6%	4%
Other	11%	10%
No metric currently being used	19%	30%

Return on capital measures show utilization rates in the mid 20 percent range. This is consistent with results earlier in the study. ERM organizations (25 percent) are more likely to use Risk Adjusted Return on Capital (RAROC) than are non-ERM organizations (16 percent). However, for Return on Capital Employed (ROCE) measures, there is little discernible difference.

The greatest disparity in terms of metrics used between ERM and non-ERM organizations is over the use of Earnings at Risk. Of the organizations with ERM, 33 percent report using this metric. This is 3.5 times higher than the nine percent of non-ERM organizations. This may be a reflection of the role earnings consistency has as a business issue.

A copy of the complete survey questionnaire and results for all respondents can be found in Appendix II.

PART II:
REPRESENTATIVE CASE STUDIES ON ENTERPRISE RISK MANAGEMENT

Summary

There are a number of organizations around the world involved in ERM to some extent. We have seen evidence of this in the literature search, the survey, and in our own experience with various client engagements. A significant aspect of this study involved interviewing leading organizations in ERM. The experiences of organizations profiled in Chapters 3 through 10 are only a sample of some of the different ways to approach ERM. It should be clear from reading the case studies that the road to ERM is very much an evolutionary process. We believe that the selected organizations provide compelling stories and some valuable lessons for both those just beginning the journey and those looking to refine their existing framework.

It was our intention, as we considered the many potential candidates to interview, to construct a set of case study organizations that provided a diverse look at trends and practices in ERM. Ultimately, we considered the following issues in making our decision:

- Participation in our benchmarking survey — and the nature of their confidential responses.
- Results from the literature search.
- Some experience operating with a full or partial ERM framework.
- Geography.
- Type of industry.
- Size of organization.
- Nominations from peers as being among leading organizations in the area of ERM.

The Institute of Internal Auditors Research Foundation

The following themes ran through the case study organizations to varying degrees:

- Most have recently gone through or are about to witness major structural change. Enhanced emphasis on risk management seems to be thought of as a way of helping deal with that scale of change.
- Several have or recently had dominant shareholders.
- Their processes gain attention internally because they are closely linked to the strategic and financial objectives of the organization.
- Key determinants of the risk management processes adopted are group structure and financial dynamics.
- Internal auditing is generally viewed as a separate department that provides independent assurance and tends not to be the main driver of risk management processes, although they are clearly involved.
- Head office risk departments tend to be small (approximately one to five people) and they are very focused on the subject of managing their enterprise risk.
- All have support from key executives (CEO or CFO); this is critical.
- They bolt their ERM framework and processes onto existing frameworks rather than create a separate framework.
- Most have adapted processes from elsewhere (primarily from various consultancies and regulatory organizations).
- The objective of the risk processes is to add value to the organization, not just provide a compliance regime.
- All look at upside as well as downside risks.
- No risk is excluded, although some (such as environmental) may be the province of other departments.
- "Risk" tends to be defined as variation from expected.

The Institute of Internal Auditors Research Foundation

CHAPTER 3
HYDRO-QUÉBEC

Overview

The Hydro-Québec case provides readers with a detailed examination of one organization's approach to ERM. In this case, readers will develop a sense of the organizational structure and resources committed to ERM, the tools used, and how ERM has evolved at Hydro-Québec. The case closes with some lessons learned from an organization that started the ERM process approximately four years ago.

Hydro-Québec

Headquarters: Montreal, Québec, Canada
Primary Industry: Electric Utilities
Internet: http://www.hyroquebec.com

2000 Data:
Annual Sales ($Mil): 8,287
Annual Assets ($Mil): 55,194
Number of employees: 17,164

Description: "Hydro-Québec is ranked among North America's largest electric utilities in terms of assets and volume of sales. The company generates, transmits, and distributes most of the electricity consumed in Québec as well as marketing and purchasing both power and energy under agreements with neighboring systems in Canada, the United States, and on spot markets. Hydro-Québec is active in energy-related research and promotion, energy transformation and conservation, and other energy-related areas. The Québec government is the single shareholder of Hydro-Québec stock." (Source: Worldscope's business description as found on www.onesource.com.)

Note: We wish to acknowledge Karen Thiessen of The Conference Board of Canada for her contribution in conducting the interview process and providing the documentation for this case.

ERM Resources at Hydro-Québec

At the end of December 1997, the ERM department was officially established as a result of several motivating as well as mitigating factors (see Figure 3.1). For the first year and a half, it focused largely on risk identification, risk processes, and in using a common risk language. In May 2000, the department had progressed to acting more like consultants to the business units. Their roles evolved to further educating the corporation on enterprise-wide risk management, and in helping to explain and quantify risk relationships.

At the present time, there are six risk counselors and one assistant, all under the leadership of the senior director. Two of the counselors are risk modeling experts and the remaining four work on processes, tools, strategic planning, and training. The senior director reports to the CFO.

Within each business unit, there is a risk coordinator who is a member of the management team. The role of these coordinators, of which there are 15, is to assist the ERM department in integrating risk management processes and communicating the required risk information — risk grids, risk maps, mitigation plans — between the business units and the ERM department. These coordinators also work on the implementation of the integrated risk process inside their business units.

Risk Policy

The mandate of the ERM department, which is explicitly written into risk policy, consists of four key tasks:

- Identify the corporation's most significant risks and present them to the board of directors twice a year.
- Design risk maps to prioritize, analyze, and monitor risks as they affect business units' objectives and corporate performance (before and after the impact of mitigation actions).
- Develop modeling/assessment tools for the business units.
- Act as a resource to the business units for risk management solutions and assist them in attaining their business objectives.

Although not formalized into policy, the ERM department does push the board of directors to regularly reassess the corporate risk tolerance. This exercise is based on the quantifiable risks the ERM department presents to the board of directors and their probability of impact on the forecasted net income.

Risk Identification Process

Identifying enterprise-wide risks within a large corporation requires a systematic process. The ERM department coordinates this process with the business units when they plan their yearly operations (usually in late fall) and when the corporation undergoes their once-every-second-year strategic planning exercise. Every other year, when the timing of these two planning exercises

Figure 3.1
Motivators Leading Hydro-Québec to ERM

■ The Board of Directors was influenced by corporate governance responsibilities and sought to maintain stakeholder value;

■ In 1997, Hydro-Québec conducted internal studies on risk management and it suggested the creation of an ERM department;

■ International markets offered opportunities, but were also offset by risks not normally encountered by Hydro-Québec, leading the company to integrate enterprise-wide risk management; and

■ The North American electrical industry was changing due to deregulation and Hydro-Québec's mission was to become more globally competitive

The Institute of Internal Auditors Research Foundation

coincide, the ERM department requests the business units to submit their top risks by summer's end.

Essentially, each business unit is required to identify, analyze, and rate the risks they face. The units also indicate which mitigation plans are already in place to deal with each major risk and which should be implemented over a five-year horizon. Finally, the units rate the risks according to impact, probability, and their mitigation plans. This is accomplished by each business unit using the risk grid developed by the ERM department.

The units submit their list of risks and corresponding analysis to the ERM department. The department then reviews and aggregates the risks to determine the top corporate risks (about 25) and graphs the probability of impact of each major risk using a risk map. The risk map is tested with different business units for feedback before a final presentation is given to the board of directors. If a risk is specific to a business unit, the ERM department will commonly use the risk analysis provided by the business unit. If the risk is common to all or many business units, the ERM department will make its own judgment on the impact and probability of that risk, based on the analysis and evaluation received from the different business units.

The board of directors and CEO decide on which risks they will focus. The business units are responsible for the development and implementation of their risk management strategies. As part of facilitating the enterprise-wide approach, the ERM department works with the business units to develop management strategies for major risks, which are common to many of the business units. The business unit(s) are responsible for strategy implementation as well as interfacing with all stakeholders and in monitoring the strategy's progress. A follow-up is conducted regularly during the year by the business units.

Evolution of the ERM Process

Hydro-Québec's first risk map was completed at the end of 1998 and presented to the board of directors in February 1999. The ERM department started with three core principles: 1) Identify the risk; 2) Evaluate the risk; and 3) Explain the risk. Since that time, the risk map has become more sophisticated in its probability ratings, but has remained fundamentally true to its original principles.

In the beginning, the priority of the ERM department was the development of a global risk map without considering any mitigation plans. With time and through experience, more sophisticated tools were developed to improve risk identification, evaluate mitigation plans, and map risks on a grid before and after the impact of mitigation plans. Please see Figure 3.2 for a sample of Hydro-Québec's 2001 Risk Analysis Form, and Figure 3.3 for a template of Hydro-Québec's Risk Map.

Figure 3.2
Hydro-Québec's Risk Analysis Form

RISK ANALYSIS FORM

Mission Statement / objectives of business unit or project	Risk	Sources	Risk Horizon (1)	Impact of Risk (2)	*Rating from 1 to 9* **Evaluation of the Gross Total Risk**		Description of Mitigation Measures (4)	Cost of Mitigation Measures (5)	*Rating from 1 to 9* **Evaluation of the Residual Risk**		Description of Residual Risk (6)
					Global Impact (3)	Probability of Occurrence (3)			Global Impact	Probability of Occurrence	

(1): Short-term: 0 to 2 years
 Intermediate term: 2 to 5 years
 Long-term: over 5 years
(2): Describe the impact(s) of the risk before mitigation measures are applied
(3): Criteria are proposed to assist in comparably evaluating the impact and probability of the risk occurring
(4): Identify the measures that can reduce or eliminate the impact(s) identified in (2). Take note that the measures can also eliminate the risk source or the probability of occurrence.
(5): Identify the financial budget (even if it is spread over several years) needed to implement the mitigation measures listed in (4), if they are not already included in the current budget
(6): Identify the residual impact(s) to which the business unit will still be exposed after having mitigated the risk

Primary purpose: Control and integration of business risks

The Institute of Internal Auditors Research Foundation

Figure 3.3
Hydro-Québec's Risk Map Template

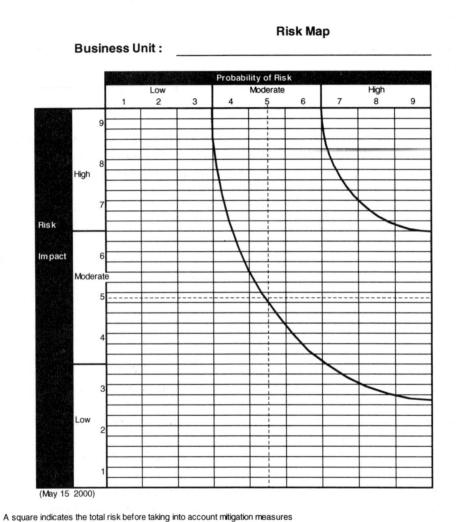

A square indicates the total risk before taking into account mitigation measures
An oval indicates the net risk after mitigation measures are applied.

R____ : _____   R____ : _____

One of the most important objectives of the ERM department for the year 2000 was to increase the corporate awareness of risk. A consultant was hired to assist in developing and facilitating risk awareness workshops. The workshops were produced in conjunction with the business units. They focused on two main questions: What is ERM and what is the value? It was followed by a simple exercise involving a group of managers to:

- Interact and define their most significant risks and determine their impact and probability ratings.
- Identify which risks are to be managed first by the business units and determine the impact of doing so on the other risks.

The end result was that the risks identified and rated earlier in the year were perhaps not as perceptively and precisely analyzed. It showed the importance of group discussion and in bringing a common understanding of all the risks and their impacts. The workshops also taught the ERM department to interact more often with the business units.

Challenges and Risks for the Near Future

As with any change management process, enterprise-wide risk management will continue to face many challenges. The ERM department, as such, has witnessed strategic, operational, regulatory, and business relationship changes that continue to affect the ERM implementation process. Some of the more challenging aspects facing the ERM department and the risks encountered by Hydro-Québec include:

- The ERM department striving for transparency — where risk evaluation methods and mitigation techniques in each business unit can be shared simultaneously.
- Improving modeling techniques.
- Prioritizing risks to the board that are significant but cannot be tangibly measured and would conceivably be considered a top corporate risk.
- Minimizing the information requests to the business units so they will continue to consult with the ERM department and not perceive it to be a priority over running their business.
- Organizational and operational changes required by the deregulation of North American electrical industry and by the introduction of a new energy board in the province of Québec.

Communication of Risks

The board of directors believes in effective and continuous communication of risks. It has supported the development of Hydro-Québec's risk policy that mandates the ERM department to effectively present and communicate the top corporate risks. Cascading the same information uniformly across the corporation continues to be a challenge. The recent risk awareness workshops, however, have paved the path in this direction. At the present time, key stakeholders such as the Québec government receive the corporation's annual reports, strategic plans, and business objectives, all of which include information on the corporation's risks. Hydro-Québec employees can visit the ERM department's Intranet site where educational information on enterprise-wide risk management can be found. Posted material includes the risk management policy, a glossary of risk terms, training courses, presentations made by team members within the organization and externally, tools for risk analysis, articles on specific kinds of risks, and links to other Web sites dedicated to risk management.

Recommendations to Enhance ERM Framework

Since the development of the ERM department, it has grown from a small unit to one that is permanently established with six risk professionals on staff. It is a department greatly appreciated by the board of directors, primarily because of its ability to quantify risks against corporate performance. It has not, however, succeeded without some lessons learned. On the contrary, their experience has brought forth many recommendations to enhance an enterprise-wide risk management framework, several of which are listed below.

- Support of CEO.
- Be aware that ERM is *not simply another strategic process,* but a collaborative mission that relies on systematic learning, education, training, and step-by-step action plans — it is a long-term commitment.
- Work first with the business units that are supportive and interested in the ERM concept, design, and implementation process. Use the success you get with those supportive units to convince the other units of the usefulness and value of ERM.
- Have the ERM department or risk coordinator act as a consultant so the corporation does not perceive it as "controlling."
- Track categories of success stories — from other industries and from within your organization — and share them with senior executives and the departments for which they are responsible.
- Meet with the CEO at least once a year and identify his/her preoccupations; then address them through the ERM program.
- Conduct a one-day session with senior executives and walk through *"what they want and where they want to go."* By the end of the session, a list of tangible goals can set the foundation for the organization's ERM strategy.
- Incorporate ERM into the corporate strategic and business planning.

CHAPTER 4
BRADFORD & BINGLEY
BUILDING SOCIETY

Overview

The Bradford & Bingley case demonstrates one organization's linkage of risk management and strategy as a key to driving shareholder value. The case also provides important insight for organizations that are considering changing corporate form (in the case of Bradford & Bingley from a mutual to stock company). The case provides an overview of the rationale, management, and oversight of the new risk process and factors included in the ERM scheme.

Bradford & Bingley Building Society

Headquarters: West Yorkshire, United Kingdom
Primary Industry: Consumer Financial Services
Internet: http://www.bradford-bingley.co.uk

2000 Data:
Annual Sales ($Mil): 2,955.5
Annual Assets ($Mil): 36,800.8
Number of employees: 8,924

Description: "Co. [Bradford & Bingley] is engaged in the provision of finance for home purchasing and improvements, commercial loans, savings and investment accounts, insurance services, the management of Personal Equity Plans and the provision of independent financial advice on a range of products regulated under the Financial Services Act, including life assurance, unit trusts and personal pensions." (Source: Mergent FIS's business description as found on www.onesource.com.)

The Institute of Internal Auditors Research Foundation

Background

History of Bradford & Bingley

Bradford & Bingley Building Society was formed in 1964 from the merger of the Bradford Equitable and the Bingley Building Societies, both originally formed in 1851. UK Building Societies are mutual organizations, equivalent in U.S. terms to savings & loan institutions. Historically, the group has provided traditional mortgage and savings products.

In April 1999, the Society announced its intention to convert from a building society to a bank listed on the London Stock Exchange. Shares began trading on December 4, 2000.

Bradford & Bingley has statutory protection from hostile takeover for five years, in that no single party can own more than 15 percent of its shares.

Major acquisitions over the past three years have been Mortgage Express (giving the organization expertise in buy-to-let mortgages and securitization) in 1997, Black Horse Estate Agencies (a real estate agency) in 1998, and John Charcol (a mortgage broker) in 2000.

Key Strengths of the Business

Bradford & Bingley has identified these key strengths:

- A clear and different strategy built around two distinct but complementary businesses: Distribution and Lending & Savings.
- A customer base of over four million customers.
- National (UK) distribution through a range of distribution channels, including approximately 600 retail outlets, online services, over 800 financial advisers, and a number of third-party distributors.
- One of the UK's largest high-street financial advisers and a leading mortgage broker.
- Flexible and profitable mortgage "manufacturing" capacity supported by outsourced mortgage processing.
- Innovative business partnerships.

Business Prospects

Bradford & Bingley's business is heavily influenced by the housing and interest rate cycles. The board has identified these key factors (effectively risk factors) for successful future performance:

- Growth through mortgage and general insurance brokering and increased sales of a wider range of wealth products.
- Continued development of online solutions.
- Focus on lending for profit, not volume.
- Management of the savings business for profit and to develop broader customer relationships.
- The retention, training, and recruitment of well-qualified employees.
- Cost reduction and investment in improved systems and processes.

Group Strategy

In developing its strategy, the board has taken into account three main market trends:

- Increasing competition from new and existing providers.
- Increased customer understanding of financial services products.
- A growing range of channels through which financial services products are being delivered.

Some quotes from Chief Executive Christopher Rodrigues illustrate the thinking behind the current group strategy.

- Describing the group's position prior to the new strategy, he said: "We were a middle-sized, retail, financial-services business. We didn't have retail scale, we didn't have manufacturing scale. We weren't even that mutual."
- Reacting to the disappointment (or worse) expressed by some analysts at the 2000 year-end results — pre-tax profits up by 2.5 percent — he said: "Frankly, we think this strategy is right on track and absolutely right for this market. Being an independent distributor and a mortgage broker and a selective lender in the middle of a mortgage price war is a pretty good place to be."

Mr. Rodrigues' goal is for 50 percent of group revenues to come from commissions on sales of other organizations' products within five years. Currently the mortgage and savings book still accounts for about 85 percent of the group's profits.

Group Services

Group-wide control and policy functions include audit, risk and compliance, group finance, human resources, and information technology.

In 1998, the group entered into agreements with IBM and British Telecom to manage and maintain part of the group's IT and telephony infrastructure.

The majority of the group's lending processing operations have also been outsourced, with Bradford & Bingley retaining 25 percent ownership of the outsourced operation. The new organization intends to generate additional income through providing mortgage processing to lenders throughout Europe.

Drivers of Risk Management

Bradford & Bingley's new approach to risk management has been driven by four factors:

- Pursuit of a radically new strategy, previously untried by any bank.
- The scale of change needed for implementation of the new strategy.
- A new stakeholder model, reflecting a broader range of stakeholders (e.g., shareholders, regulators, and commercial partners).
- Compliance with:
  - Corporate governance requirements (Turnbull reporting).
  - Bank regulatory requirements.
  - London Stock Exchange listing requirements.

The board therefore decided that a more robust framework would be required for managing risk. This thinking explains the new role of group risk and the new mandate for internal auditing.

Criteria of Success

Group risk has identified these three key requirements for successful management of risk:

- Consistency of message/language: in internal as well as external communications. "Risk" is defined as variation from stakeholder expectations.
- An internal control framework: this should cover every aspect from board delegation of its authority through to management processes in the businesses.
- A balanced scorecard to reflect how the strategy is being implemented and to drive performance.

Once these three are in place, the link to Bradford & Bingley's strategy will have become clear and risk management will have become embedded into the businesses' processes. Figure 4.1 (developed by group risk) describes the link between each of the above three components and the rewards from achieving them.

Roles and Responsibilities in Management of Risk

The group risk and group internal auditing functions both report to a main board director.

The board has delegated oversight of risk to its Audit, Risk, and Compliance Committee, which is made up of non-executive directors and chaired by the vice chairman. Group risk and group internal audit provide regular reports to this committee, although each function has responsibility for both identifying and managing its own risks.

The group's Risk Management Committee, made up of executive managers, is chaired by a main board director who is also the company secretary.

The head of group risk has three broad accountabilities:

- Ensuring the group does not suffer material loss through lack of a risk management framework.
- Adding value through developing risk as an enabling function.
- Development of the framework for assessment/management of risk and people to lead the management of risk.

Internal auditing provides independent and objective assurance that the risk framework is robust enough to do what it is supposed to do. The criteria used for this assessment are:

- Adequacy of design.
- Effectiveness of its operation.

Group internal auditing is a long established function, but its current head was brought in with a mandate for change, reflecting the strategic aspirations of Bradford & Bingley and the general wish of regulators to upgrade the quality of risk management in the context of change from building society to bank status. He was therefore asked to reengineer the vision for the function, its positioning, and its activity. Internal auditing is now moving well away from the traditional periodic audit toward regular updates on critical control points.

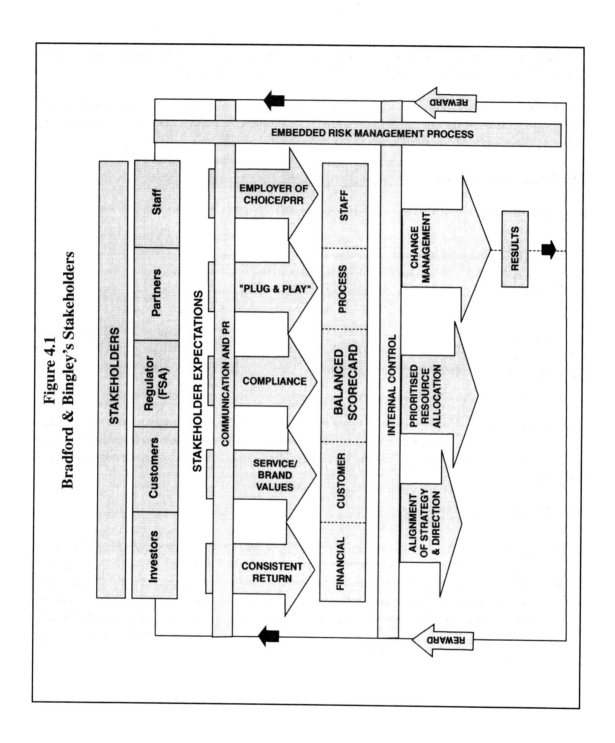

Figure 4.1
Bradford & Bingley's Stakeholders

Internal auditing wants to harmonize and integrate the agenda, systems of reporting, and language used by group risk and internal auditing with those used in the businesses.

Group risk and internal auditing have reviewed risk management processes and whether they will meet the objectives described above. So far they have established that the processes comply with objectives, but still have to demonstrate how their roles can add value to the group.

The Chain of Responsibility

Bradford & Bingley's four broad categories of risk are:

- Financial.
- Operational.
- Strategic.
- External.

Financial risk is divided into credit and market risk. The head of balance sheet risk looks after market risk and reports to the Asset Liability Committee. There is a separate head of credit risk reporting to the Credit Risk Committee. The head of group risk sits on both of these committees but is chairman of neither.

Most activities of the Audit Risk & Compliance Committee and the Risk Management Committee have so far been concerned with the three non-financial risk areas, which are more to do with achievement of the new strategy, and therefore focus on the bank's new distribution and intermediary role.

Risk Management Methodologies

- Market risk: Bradford & Bingley is considering moving to a Value-at-Risk (VAR) methodology to allow greater automation and monitoring of liquidity on a day-by-day basis.
- Credit risk: The risk is assessed separately for each portfolio (e.g., the residential portfolio, commercial portfolio, etc.). Within each portfolio the loan-to-value ratio is monitored and a high/medium/low basis of scoring riskiness is used. A more sophisticated methodology is being put in place in order to maximize value from assets in the portfolio (e.g., looking for upside risk opportunities).

- Operational risk: Group risk is looking to introduce a means of ranking risks, according to the scale of threat they represent to achievement of corporate objectives. Ideally, real time updating of the scale of threat for the "top 10" risks would be possible. Until "a tool" is found for this, self-assessment workshops are a primary source of information on risks. Issues of "ownership" and "treatment" are flushed out during workshop sessions. Therefore, each business now has "risk owners" and "risk treatment owners."

Impact and likelihood of each risk are tracked on a two-dimensional matrix (impact vs. likelihood). Processes exist to ensure that other risks are managed on a day-to-day basis by the business.

Examples of risks managed by the business, rather than being in the "top 10," are:

- IT system availability.
- Levels of rework.

The whole process is designed to ensure that risks are being captured and treated at the most appropriate level.

How this Approach was Determined

The Risk Committee had considered a number of different proposals from various organizations prior to the arrival of the current head of group risk. Various parts of processes offered by two major firms of consultants were selected and adapted to Bradford & Bingley's requirements. The board realized it was more important, for achieving real change, to develop processes internally, rather than asking an external consultant to come in and review the current approach and recommend an alternative. The processes are therefore not a branded product but unique to Bradford & Bingley.

Communication

The head of group risk regularly briefs Bradford & Bingley's senior managers on the "top 10" risks to achieving the group strategy.

Information on the "top 10" risks will be shared quite widely, so that all staff can see how their work contributes to management of those risks. However, it is still unclear whether "pull" or "push" methods of communication are best for this purpose. An Intranet portal for risk issues is being considered as a possible way of making the information widely accessible. Whatever the method, transparency is being demanded by staff, regulators, and investors alike. It is part of the job of group risk to ensure that a common language and understanding is developed among all stakeholders.

Ultimately, the head of group risk wants information on the key risks to be accessible also to outsiders. He also wants to be able to test the sensitivity of the bank's strategy and results to different risks. At the moment these are aspirations rather than reality.

Key Challenges

A critical challenge is delivery of the balanced scorecard (see Figure 4.1). Design of it is crucial. Getting buy-in from the chief executive, now achieved, is a critical first step.

It is also recognized that a major shift in culture is needed among Bradford & Bingley staff after 150 years working as a mutual organization to align them with the re-branding about to happen as part of the bank's new strategy as a distributor. The rules, regulations, and codes of best practice, which come with Bradford & Bingley's new status, help to drive change in the culture.

The Future

Bradford & Bingley's management recognizes that it is engaged in an unproven strategy: either the strategy works, which will make it attractive to other organizations, or, if the strategy is seen to fail, the independent future of the group will be under question. It is still not clear how the stock market will value Bradford & Bingley in the medium term.

Demonstrating the potential value of the new strategy within the next three years depends on the delivery of effective risk management systems.

CHAPTER 5
AUSTRALIAN COMMUNICATIONS COMPANY

Overview

This case provides readers with an overview of an Australian Communications Company (the actual name of the company is not identified per the client's request) that links risk management to operations. This case provides examples of internal communication tools and reports and coordination of risk management for an organization that views understanding key risks as a prerequisite for outstanding management.

Australian Communications Company

Headquarters: Australia
Primary Industry: Communications Services

2000 Data:
Annual Sales ($Mil): >500
Annual Assets ($Mil): >500
Number of employees: >2,000

Background

Since its establishment in the early 1990s, this Australian communications company has embraced the concept of enterprise risk management (ERM). Although the term "Enterprise Risk Management" is not used within the organization, management recognized early on that managing the organization's global risks was an essential building block to a successful business operation. Perhaps a better description of their approach to the process is the appropriate management of the range of risks (and their interaction) underlying the organization's operations.

Current Risk Management Framework

The framework and risk policies have changed little over the organization's history. The role of the risk manager is one of all-encompassing facilitation of risk management activity. Specialists in security, environmental issues, business continuity, risk auditing, and contractual risk report directly to the risk manager, who is also accountable for the adequacy of risk management policies (including treasury and finance activities). The risk manager reports to the finance director.

There is no "Risk Management Board" as such, but a Management Operating Committee, comprising the CEO, deputy CEO, and six other directors. This committee is accountable to the board, which has ultimate responsibility for risk management.

The risk manager provides a fortnightly "Flash Report" to the board that deals with ongoing matters on outstanding issues from the previous report and raises any new issues. Additionally, he or she gives regular feedback sessions to the board, each with a specific focus. For example, a future session is planned around the issue of criticality analysis — on the need to establish the important requirements for each new system or site of activity.

There is no one "champion" of risk management activity, since it is important that each function of the organization has its own "champion director." Another aspect of the risk manager's facilitation role, therefore, is to ensure that each function in the organization identifies a director to take responsibility for identifying and managing risk. The entire process has been helped by the fact that senior management has elevated the whole issue of risk management, particularly the organization's first CEO and finance director, and subsequent finance directors.

Risk Identification and Analysis

Part of the underlying fabric of the organization's operations is that new and changing risks are identified as an integral feature of the organization's management function. The risk manager, with assistance from specialists, ensures that such risks are fully and accurately identified and understood, so that the appropriate risk management response can take place.

One key to successful implementation is the recognition that only a manageable (small) number of focus areas need to be defined. As an example, the organization's initial focus was ensuring that the "customer was king." This meant that risk management was focused on seeing that customer service was of the highest possible quality (i.e., security, network, financial, billing, etc.).

The organization uses an internal communication tool called the Business Impact Analysis Report to concentrate on a simple range of key needs associated with each new, or changing, activity. This does not mean that the approach to risk analysis is simplistic. On the contrary, complex analysis often underlies each key issue.

An important requirement of the continuing appropriateness and success of the risk management approach is the continuing update by the risk manager of his or her understanding of, and influence on, the organization's risk appetite as well as the spread of changing and new risks. This is achieved through ongoing interactions with the appropriate senior executives and during workshops where necessary. This all helps provide an evolutionary approach to the risk as the organization's culture and risk philosophy changes.

Business, and the way it is done, is changing rapidly, and at an accelerating rate, for the organization. This presents new areas of ownership of risk and changing areas of ownership. For instance, there are changes in technology that feed the organization's core delivery of services and changes in regulation of its activities. This calls for increasing focus on the need for facilitation of the risk management process.

Success Factors

The main recommendation for the smooth and full application of risk management overall is to retain a close focus on the ongoing key issues for the business — linked with an understanding of the main risks underlying these issues. This can only be achieved by a continual process of updating the understanding and management of the organization's risk framework through consistent interactions with key members of the organization. Another key success factor has been the support from senior management. As seen in many of the other case studies, high-level executive support is a must.

CHAPTER 6
CLARICA LIFE INSURANCE

Overview

The Clarica case provides readers with an example of an organization that decided to use risk management as a strategic, competitive asset. An ERM framework provided the organization with greater confidence in assessing and understanding risk and allowed it to raise its risk tolerance through better insights into the risk/return tradeoffs.

Clarica also provides readers with an excellent example of how the organization instituted the plan internally and its overall communication strategy regarding its ERM framework. The case ends with several lessons taken from Clarica's experience.

Clarica Life Insurance Co.

Headquarters: Waterloo, Ontario, Canada
Primary Industry: Insurance (Life)
Internet: http://www.clarica.com

2000 Data:
Annual Sales ($Mil): 2,480
Annual Assets ($Mil): 22,058
Number of employees: 7,300

Description: "Co. [Clarica] is a diversified financial services organization. Co. offers a range of customized products and services: (i) retail insurance provides a range of life insurance products to over 1.5 million individual policyholders; (ii) the savings & retirement segment provides annuities, GICs, and an assortment of mutual funds and segregated funds; (iii) group insurance provides employee benefit solutions to corporations and small businesses throughout Canada; (iv) the surplus segment includes Canadian investment management and corporate operations; and (v) the U.S. insurance and savings segment which offers wealth accumulation and financial security solutions to target markets in the United States through life insurance and annuity products. In addition, Co. offers reinsurance operations, managed as part of the U.S. branch. The branch's operations are divided into two lines of reinsurance business: life retrocession and special risk reinsurance." (Source: Mergent FIS's business description as found on www.onesource.com.)

The Institute of Internal Auditors Research Foundation

Getting Started with ERM

Clarica's ERM framework has evolved through time, but traces its roots back to 1997 with an internal initiative called "Financial Management Strategy." This strategy focused on the stability and quality of Clarica's earnings and dealt with various performance and financial issues, including the management of risk. Clarica's internal assessment of the state of risk management in 1997 indicated it was inefficiently fragmented among various business units and specialties. In the process of articulating their future strategy, Clarica realized that they eventually needed to integrate their overall approach to managing risk.

In 1999, after completing the process of demutualization, Clarica began to think again about their overall risk framework. They assembled a cross-functional, internal team at both the steering committee and working group levels to develop Clarica's ERM framework. They received support from both the CFO and chief investment officer and they worked closely with a consultant to develop an overall strategy and approach.

In the fall of 1999, the working group began to gather data to update their understanding of the current state of risk management. They interviewed several members of Clarica's top management and conducted an internal survey of approximately 100 people to better understand the risks facing their organization and how these risks were being managed. They also solicited ideas from interviewees and survey participants about what the future of risk management at Clarica should look like.

Once all the data had been analyzed, the working group coordinated with the steering committee to articulate a business vision and framework for their ERM program. They created the following ERM mission statement:

> *"An integrated process for identifying, measuring, and monitoring the risk/return tradeoffs in all aspects of Clarica's business to enable a culture of informed decision-making and risk/return optimization."*

The framework they designed is discussed under a separate heading below. This entire project took about 10 weeks to complete and they have been in the process of implementing and refining the framework since that time.

Clarica took a rather pragmatic and measured approach to implementing their ERM framework. Initially there was some resistance to the initiative when it came to the availability of resources. Because of this pushback, the working group decided to focus on areas with a quick payback —

hoping that small wins would demonstrate the value of ERM and help muster future support. They first focused their efforts on the market and credit risks in their investment and reinsurance business units. These were big issues and they had data on these risks readily available. They felt they had a better understanding of these risks and believed they could make better decisions around these issues that would provide a quick payback. For Clarica, it was about getting the best risk-related return.

Key Drivers of ERM

The working group discovered through their internal research that Clarica had tended to be risk averse as an organization. They concluded that Clarica could improve returns by taking more risks. However, they wanted to be deliberate about their risk taking, which required improving their existing framework for measuring capital and the risks *of* and *to* the business — and understanding where to invest in the business. This need was a key driver in developing their ERM framework.

It is interesting to note that major losses/catastrophes (either their own or those in their industry) did not factor heavily into Clarica's decision to embark on ERM. Instead, they were motivated by the desire to improve the quality and level of Clarica's sustainable earnings.

Another key catalyst to Clarica's ERM framework implementation was the process of becoming a publicly held stock company in July 1999. Clarica had been a mutual insurance company since its founding nearly 130 years earlier. The demutualization process involved a great deal of change, and with this change came the recognition by many managers that they had to be more deliberate about taking risk than they had in the past to get better returns. ERM was positioned as a value-added tool to help Clarica achieve better returns through improved understanding and management of risk.

Clarica's ERM Framework

Clarica recognized early in the process of implementing ERM that people generally knew about most of the risks in their specific line of business. However, because their past approach to identifying, prioritizing, and treating risk was fragmented among various business units and specialties, they lacked a common way of talking about the risks.

Clarica's ERM framework helps alleviate this problem by providing a more uniform way of categorizing and measuring risk. This enables managers to identify and focus on risks across a broader spectrum than was previously possible. At a high level, Clarica's ERM framework consists of nine principles, seven key elements, and six risk types.

Principles of ERM Framework

- Maximize shareholder value
- Articulate and communicate risk profile
- Optimize the whole portfolio
- Look forward
- Create a risk/return culture
- Make risk understandable
- Make risk comparable
- Maintain flexibility
- Enhance business model

Elements of ERM Framework

- A target risk profile
- A risk/return culture
- A common language (six risk categories — see the section below on Categories of Risk within ERM Framework for more information)
- A common currency (economic capital and risk adjusted return on capital)
- An integrated risk management unit
- Policies and limits
- An enterprise risk/capital report (see the section below on Risk Communication to Stakeholders for more information)

The element of Clarica's ERM framework dealing with a common currency (a proprietary model based on economic capital and risk-adjusted return on capital) has evolved module-by-module. For example, they've done work on market and credit risk (the quick wins they were looking for) and are currently working on the insurance and operational modules.

Categories of Risk within ERM Framework

Risk awareness is the recognition and understanding of all forms of risk to which Clarica is exposed. Management needs to be fully aware of the risks that Clarica is undertaking or it cannot minimize the downside and maximize the upside within its risk appetite. Part of this awareness is the development of a common language for risk.

At Clarica, there are six main categories of risk. They are business risk, insurance risk, credit risk, market risk, operational risk, and organizational risk. Each of these main categories is further defined into subcategories.

- **Business Risk:** The uncertainty about financial outcomes due to changes in product volumes and margins. Specific business risks are:
  - Strategy risk: the risk that arises from choosing strategies, business models, or implementation plans.
  - Infrastructure risk: the risk that the existing system infrastructure will not be able to support strategic business initiatives.
  - Customer risk: the risk that unsound sales practices or poor service quality will hurt customer retention and new business generation.
  - Product risk: the risk associated with product design and pricing, including the ability to identify target markets and properly price for policyholder behavior. It is also the risk of not pricing properly for the embedded risks within a product.
  - Competitive risk: the risks and opportunities that arise from the actions and reactions of key competitors, which may directly result in volatility in sales volume, premium and fee levels, and input costs.
  - Regulatory risk: the risk of regulatory changes that affect Clarica's business, including products, capital requirements, or taxation.
  - Reputation risk: the risk of engaging in any activities or practices that could affect public perception of Clarica's image and brand. Reputation risk often results from mismanagement of other risks.

- **Insurance Risk**: The uncertainty about financial outcomes due to differences between the actual and expected amount of claims and benefit payments. Specific insurance risks are:
  - Mortality risk: the risk of misestimating how long policyholders will live resulting in higher-than-expected claims and benefit payments.
  - Morbidity risk: the risk of misestimating the number of times a policyholder will be sick or the length of the illness, resulting in higher-than-expected claims and benefit payments.
  - Lapse risk: the risk of misestimating lapse rates in product pricing decisions.

- **Credit Risk**: The uncertainty about financial outcomes surrounding default likelihood. Specific credit risks are:
  - Issuer risk: the risk of a credit instrument's issuer failing to meet their financial obligations.
  - Lending risk: the risk of a borrower defaulting.
  - Counter-party risk: the risk of guarantors or reinsurers being unable to back their guarantee.

The Institute of Internal Auditors Research Foundation

- **Market Risk**: The uncertainty about financial outcomes arising from changes in market prices or indices. Specific market risks are:
  - Interest rate risk: the risk of asset-liability mismatch resulting from interest rate volatility.
  - Liquidity risk: the risk of being unable to meet financial obligations as they come due.
  - Foreign exchange risk: the risk of foreign exchange rate fluctuations.
  - Equity risk: the risk of stock price fluctuations.
  - Basis risk: the risk of a hedge becoming less effective due to a change in the normal relationship between two floating rates.
  - Real estate risk: the risk of real estate value fluctuations.

- **Operational Risk**: The uncertainty about financial outcomes arising from events caused by failures in people, process, and technology, as well as external dependencies. Specific operational risks are:
  - Processing risk: the risk of human or system error within a certain process or transaction.
  - Control risk: the risk of non-compliance with established business guidelines, policies, or limits.
  - System risk: the risk of information systems, communication systems, or computer systems failing.
  - Model risk: the risk of using inappropriate assumptions or methodologies in constructing models, tools, or systems.
  - Fraud risk: the risk of theft or intentional mismanagement of company assets or information by an employee or third party.
  - Compliance risk: the risk of nonconformance with laws, rules, regulations, prescribed practices, or ethical standards in any jurisdiction in which Clarica operates.
  - Legal risk: the risk of legal action resulting in costly legal fees, fines, or settlements.
  - Information security risk: the risk of inadequately protecting confidential information from employees, competitors, and the public.
  - External disruption risk: the risk of loss resulting from external events such as natural disasters, terrorism, or the failure of the public infrastructure.

- **Organizational Risk**: The uncertainty about financial outcomes relating to the company's structure and capabilities. It pertains specifically to the company's capability to implement business strategies and effectively manage the operations of the company. Specific organizational risks are:
  - People risk: the risk of being unable to attract and retain employees with the appropriate skills, experience, or ethics.

The Institute of Internal Auditors Research Foundation

- Incentive risk: the risk of incentive programs inadequately rewarding performance compared to competitors or motivating employees to make inappropriate business decisions or behave unethically.
- Cultural risk: the risk of not linking the corporate culture with the company's risk and return objectives or not communicating the culture throughout the organization.
- Change management risk: the risk of not adapting to or meeting key organizational initiatives because of resistance, lack of resources, improper scoping, or poor implementation plans.

ERM Structure

Clarica has taken a somewhat decentralized approach to ERM. The organizational structure might best be described as an umbrella with several functions beneath it (see Figure 6.1). Clarica's corporate risk management department has overall accountability for the measurement and monitoring of the complete set of risks facing the organization. Its general role is to help provide the framework, the tools, and the resources. Underneath this layer, at the functional level, are the Investment Risk Management Office, Corporate Auditing Services, and the various business unit (BU) actuarial teams.

The Investment Risk Management Office has direct accountability for the management of credit and market risk inherent in Clarica's asset base. Corporate Auditing Services is focused primarily on the identification and mitigation of risk exposures for the business, operational, and organizational risk categories. Finally, the business unit actuarial teams have primary accountability for the measurement and monitoring of insurance-related risks and work with the product development and pricing teams to ensure risk is identified and appropriately managed.

The current head of the ERM effort, Karen Higgins, is a part of the internal auditing (IA) team and reports to Doug Brooks, the appointed actuary. Ms. Higgins' three-member team has accountability across the board when it comes to economic capital, operational risk, risk management education/communication, and a variety of project management, continuity planning, and insurance risk management issues. She devotes half of her time to leading this team and advancing ERM across the organization.

The appointed actuary's role is to incorporate risk management in all aspects of financial management, including the valuation of liabilities, planning, financial management strategy, financial reporting, auditing, and capital management. The actuary reports to the CFO.

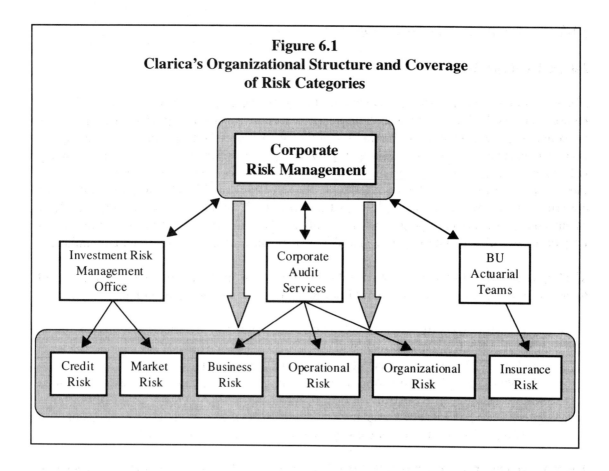

Figure 6.1
Clarica's Organizational Structure and Coverage of Risk Categories

The IA function has specific accountabilities for assessing operational risk and, to a lesser extent, organizational and business risk. The IA function does not play an active role in the measurement of risk, but monitors and reports on the implementation of solutions to deal with the identified risks.

The corporate risk management team meets regularly and they are in the process of formulating a Cross-Clarica Risk Committee (part of the next evolutionary step scheduled for 2001). This committee's expected role is to identify risk issues, evaluate what's happening in risk management across Clarica in general, and determine how business units are involved in risk management. The individuals on the team have the support of their respective vice presidents and the CFO serves as an executive-level champion of the entire effort.

Risk Communication to Stakeholders

Internal Stakeholders

Clarica's primary method for communicating to senior managers about the key risks affecting their business is the Capital and Risk Report. Clarica believes that the Capital and Risk Report is an example of a best practice tool because it addresses risk from both an educational and operational perspective. For example, the report provides specific information to managers about key risks in each business unit and the firm's capital structure, helps reinforce the common measurement of risk, and serves as both a reference and educational tool. It also helps to portray the concept that risk has an upside and not just a downside. Team members from Corporate Risk Management, IA, and the appointed actuary's office collaborate to generate this report on a quarterly basis. It is distributed to upper and middle management as well as to the audit committee.

The Capital and Risk Report is organized into three primary sections. The first section is organized by business unit and includes a number of useful features for managers, including:

- Examples of emerging areas of potential risk exposure (e.g., segregated fund guarantees).
- Discussions on key topics such as their embedded value initiative.
- A chart of Clarica's capital structure and how it has changed by risk type.
- A display of the key operational, organizational, and business risks within each business unit, including a color-coded indicator of the severity of the risk (low, moderate, or high) and how it has changed compared to the previous quarter. This display also includes a brief narrative description of the key risks and the rationale for the ranking.

The next section of the report is called the Risk Event Log. Its purpose is to share information about what risk events were identified, what impact they had or could have had, and what was done to mitigate the downside risk. The emphasis of this section of the report is primarily educational in that it disseminates information about risk management best practices. The vice presidents of each area provide the underlying information for this section of the report on a quarterly basis.

The last section of the report is strictly educational and includes a discussion of various hot topics. For example, a recent report discussed the topic of economic capital and included a glossary.

The management of Clarica also provides periodic updates on risk management issues to the audit committee of the board and outlines their overall financial management strategy, including their plans for the upcoming year and what has been accomplished.

The Institute of Internal Auditors Research Foundation

External Stakeholders

Stock analysts. Discussions about risk with analysts have tended to focus on particular topics of interest to the analysts. For example, in a recent conference call Clarica's management addressed how they manage credit risk and outlined where they see it going and how they're positioned to react to their credit exposures. Clarica has also provided information about its ERM framework to analysts and to the Toronto Stock Exchange.

Regulators. The Office of the Superintendency of Financial Institutions (OSFI) wants Clarica and other organizations to have solid risk management policies. They want the organization to be well managed, but OSFI has limited resources to auditing practices. Clarica has communicated to OSFI what they have done in the area of risk management and what they intend to do during 2001. They have also provided regulators with sample copies of their Capital and Risk Report. OSFI has been supportive and receptive, but they are not ready to make any changes to their regulatory capital formula at this point.

Shareholders. When Clarica's management talks with shareholders about risk they tend to do so in general terms — discussing how they manage risk factors such as market, credit, and liquidity risks. They also describe their overall risk profile to shareholders by outlining where they do and don't take risks — either in terms of how they invest capital or underwrite their products. Clarica primarily attempts to communicate these issues in a section of the annual report, but they still hope to make improvements in how they align the risk language with their framework.

Future Plans

As mentioned previously, operational risk is slated for 2001 as the next module of focus. Clarica plans to tackle operational risk from a top down approach beginning with a pilot project of a specific area. They plan to run through an operational risk scorecard and use data from the selected business area to identify specific performance drivers. They expect operational risk will be more difficult to measure than the other areas they've addressed so far (market, credit, and insurance), because they feel this area brings with it a sort of inherent subjectivity. However, they don't want the perceived subjectivity of operational risk to prevent them from looking at it and applying their methodology to these risks.

Clarica's Keys to Success — and Cautions

When asked to describe things that worked well as they have implemented ERM, as well as some of the lessons learned, Clarica identified the following keys to success and added some cautionary notes.

- Having leaders who are passionate about this subject is a must.
- Formulating the strategy, then the framework, and then phasing it in using a modular approach.
- Building the business case by demonstrating that they had a greater risk tolerance than they were exploiting, and if they exploited it, they could increase returns with few adverse consequences.
- Ensuring that a balanced approach is taken by focusing on those risk areas where they believe the greatest payback exists.
- Trying not to do too much at once. They have an aggressive plan for 2001 and they have a lot of talent in the corporate risk management team. It will be a challenge to keep them grounded.
- Continuing to keep the message out there. They hope the establishment of the Cross-Clarica Risk Committee will help accomplish this.

CHAPTER 7
KEYCORP

Overview

This case profiles the evolutionary experience of a large U.S.-based bank with its ERM program. It describes how incremental improvements to the ERM process, framework, and their organizational structure have resulted from formal organizational reviews. This case also discusses the role of capital allocation and introduces the concept of tying management compensation programs with the risk and capital allocation framework. The case concludes with several practical recommendations for other organizations involved in ERM.

KeyCorp

Headquarters: Cleveland, Ohio
Primary Industry: Commercial Banks
Internet: http://www.key.com

2000 Data:
Annual Sales/Revenue ($Mil): 8,471
Annual Assets ($Mil): 87,270.0
Number of Employees: 22,142

Description: "KeyCorp is an integrated multi-line financial services company... KeyCorp's subsidiaries provide a wide range of investment management, retail and commercial banking, consumer finance, and investment banking products and services to corporate, individual, and institutional clients through four lines of business: Key Retail Banking, Key Specialty Finance, Key Corporate Capital, and Key Capital Partners." (Source: Market guide business description as found on www.onesource.com.)

Beginnings of ERM at KeyCorp

KeyCorp's experience with ERM has been an evolutionary process driven by a number of internal and external factors. Internally, it has been driven by the desire to continually improve the job of risk management. For example, they recognized early on that there were advantages to combining and coordinating their various risk management disciplines. Previously, these disciplines had been fragmented among various specialties such as market risk, credit risk, and audit and compliance risk. External factors influencing the development of KeyCorp's ERM framework include corporate governance initiatives (e.g., COSO document and program) and regulatory compliance pressures (e.g., Basle Committee). Combined, these factors have led to incremental changes to KeyCorp's ERM program, including organizational realignments and adjustments to their capital allocation system.

Many of the ideas for improvements in KeyCorp's ERM framework have resulted from periodic, formal organizational reviews. During the course of these reviews different project teams evaluate the entire organization and generate ideas for improvement. Subsequently, some of these ideas advance to the highest executive committees for review. Once the ideas are accepted and adopted into the framework, management implements the appropriate changes.

As mentioned above, KeyCorp's approach to risk had been fragmented among various risk disciplines. KeyCorp made the decision a few years ago, through the organizational review process, to have all of the risk disciplines report to one executive — the Risk Czar. The Risk Czar was the predecessor to the current chief risk officer (CRO) position at KeyCorp. At the same time they realigned the organizational structure along business lines rather than by risk discipline. They believed this arrangement would create synergies and provide more comprehensive risk services — or "one-stop shopping" to the business lines.

However, implementing incremental changes such as the organizational realignment described above has been a challenge. The biggest hurdles have primarily involved issues related to organizational culture. Simply put, people get accustomed to a certain system or way of doing things and sometimes find it difficult to change. This was more the case within the risk management disciplines than the business lines. In time they have made significant progress in overcoming many of the organizational culture barriers, but there is still work to be done.

Capital Allocation

A key component of KeyCorp's ERM program involves capital allocation. As an organization, KeyCorp offers a variety of products and services across several business lines. This complicates the evaluation of their disparate business activities and risks on an "apples-to-apples" basis. They feel their capital allocation system is an effective way to achieve this comparison. The capital allocation system is also used to evaluate the risk-adjusted return of new products, services, and lines of business. Overall, their capital allocation system helps them determine where they should invest resources and expand and where they are not getting the appropriate return for their money.

The development and fine-tuning of their capital allocation system is driven by a desire to make better decisions about their business and decrease earnings volatility and also by regulatory pressures. KeyCorp and other large banks, both in the U.S. and internationally, recognize that ultimately they will either end up with an effective industry-developed methodology for capital allocation or a regulatory one. An industry methodology is preferable to KeyCorp, because there is the risk that a regulatory one might be arbitrary and put them at a competitive disadvantage in certain lines of business.

KeyCorp expects that one of the benefits of implementing ERM will be decreased volatility in their earnings. In the process of capital allocation, the volatility of expenses and earnings plays a major role. For example, a business line with volatile earnings will typically require more allocated capital than one that has steady, but not necessarily spectacular, results. By having a better capital allocation system they hope to make better decisions about where to put their money for the best risk-adjusted returns — and decrease their earnings volatility.

KeyCorp utilizes two primary metrics in the process of measuring the net risk for each business unit and in allocating capital to the business lines. They use Value at Risk (VAR) for their investment products and for the brokerage business. VAR is a measurement system commonly used by financial services organizations to monitor the risks associated with their trading activity. The second metric measurement involves the use of probability of default (POD) and loss given default (LGD) on its credit portfolios. VAR, POD, and LGD serve as primary devices of capital attribution for market and credit risk.

KeyCorp's ERM Structure

KeyCorp's ERM activities are led and coordinated at the highest level by a risk council made up of a number of senior executives, including the chairman and CEO. The risk council is chaired by the CRO. Meetings are scheduled on an ad hoc basis depending on the need to manage any new and significant emerging risk issues, but typically take place every month or every other month. The risk council makes decisions about how the organization will position itself relative to the risks it faces.

A significant item discussed during a recent risk council meeting was integrating the capital allocation system to the incentive system. KeyCorp is developing a single model that ties the incentive plans to the capital allocation system. This represents an important evolutionary step in KeyCorp's ERM process. Once completed, it is expected that incentives will be tied to some extent on how well risks are managed. It will take approximately a year to implement the integrated program, but KeyCorp estimates that creating a linkage between these two systems will improve overall results for the organization.

The organizational structure and processes are all designed to help support the capital allocation system. As explained earlier, KeyCorp has organized the risk disciplines, including the internal auditing function, along key business segments. For example, one group provides complete risk management services to the entire capital markets investment business. Any auditing or anything to do with credit risk or compliance is headed up by one individual. Another individual heads up the retail consumer banking function and provides the same type of service. These individuals report to the CRO and are responsible for, among other things, determining the net risk of their respective units for each of the following risk categories:

- Credit.
- Market.
- Operational.
- Technology.
- Compliance.

KeyCorp's general auditor reports to the CRO and has responsibilities for compliance in the deposit arena, including money laundering, ATMs, and other electronic products. Physical security and other security generalists also report to him. Overall, the general auditor must ensure that the internal auditing function embedded in those components is active and functioning well and that the auditing specialists contained within other risk management units are knowledgeable, qualified, current, and actively performing their duties.

Risk Communication

The method and timing of risk communication varies among internal stakeholders. For example, risk exposures measured using VAR, as described above, are communicated to certain business lines on a daily basis. However, KeyCorp only communicates VAR trends to its directors approximately every other month. On a more general level, KeyCorp produces an annual risk profile report for its directors. This report discusses the risk profile of the main parts of the business, whether the risks are increasing or decreasing, and how well they are being managed.

KeyCorp's primary method for communicating about risk issues to external stakeholders is the annual report. For example, they address the responsibilities of the audit and risk management committee. They discuss VAR measures and the degree of exposure, how they monitor that exposure, and the positions they have. They used to focus more on risks associated with financial derivatives in the annual report, but this emphasis has diminished for two reasons. First, the markets are much better developed, and second, the methodologies and the expertise for controlling derivatives-based risk have improved tremendously for most organizations. Within the annual report, KeyCorp also describes the main lines of business, their performance, and their risk-adjusted return.

Future Plans

Key Corp expects their ERM process to continually evolve and improve in the future. In the near term they are focused on cross-training employees to help build a broad risk perspective among their staff. As described earlier, they also hope to improve the linkage between the entire risk management review process, the capital allocation system, and the incentive plans for each business unit.

KeyCorp is also planning to improve their quantification and management of operational risks. This is a challenging area at the moment, particularly when it comes to capital allocation. KeyCorp hopes that their participation in various data-sharing consortiums will help lead to the development of an effective approach to operational risk.

There are some other potential concerns on the horizon for KeyCorp that may impact their ERM framework. For example, there is some concern about the possible impact of pronouncements from the various regulatory bodies. There is uncertainty about what will they pronounce, what demands they will have with respect to capital allocation, and what systems they will accept. KeyCorp hopes that the framework, processes, and organizational structure they have already established will put them in a good position to react to any regulatory requirements.

Recommendations

We asked KeyCorp, based on their experience with ERM, to provide some practical recommendations to organizations that are just beginning — or in the process of refining — an ERM framework. While some of their recommendations listed below may apply more specifically to organizations in the financial services industry (e.g., capital allocation), we feel they provide valuable insights for a wide variety of organizations.

- Have a senior-level executive (e.g., Risk Czar/CRO) coordinate and champion a good risk management system.
- Develop a philosophy where "everybody owns the risk."

- Establish and continually improve a good capital allocation system as a decision-making tool. This is especially important if you have a diverse product/service offering. An effective capital allocation system helps provide an "apples-to-apples" comparison of the various products/services and determine where you should put more (or less) of your money in the future. Capital allocation also assists in achieving the "Holy Grail" of risk management — determining if you are being rewarded for the risk you take.
- Create a linkage between incentives and the management of risk.
- Be prepared for the change process to take a good deal of time and effort, especially among individual practitioners in the risk disciplines.

CHAPTER 8
INFINEON TECHNOLOGIES AG

Overview

The Infineon case provides readers with an overview of the use of ERM from a corporate perspective as well as in the critical function of revenue forecasting. The case shows how Infineon uses risk management as a tool for assisting in better understanding its forecasts and as a means for helping managers understand the issues that can cause forecasts to be missed. The case also identifies key challenges to implementing ERM across a broad range of core business processes.

Infineon Technologies AG

Headquarters: Munich, Germany
Primary Industry: Semiconductors
Internet: http://www.infineon.com

2000 Data:
Annual Sales ($Mil): 6.436
Annual Assets ($Mil): 8,160
Number of Employees: 29,000

Description: "Infineon AG was founded in 1999 as a spin-off from Siemens and was listed on the stock exchange in March 2000. The company is one of the top 10 manufacturers of semiconductors in the world. The company manufactures digital, mixed-signal, and analog integrated circuits for the communications, automotive, computer, security, chip card, and other industries." The company consists of five business units: wireline products, wireless products, security and chip card products, automotive and industrial, and memory products. (Source: Adapted from Worldscope's business description as found on www.onesource.com.)

Background to ERM at Infineon

The approach to ERM at Infineon is ultimately linked to its business objectives and forecasting process. It has also been driven by corporate governance initiatives and has been influenced by its history as part of Siemens AG. To provide some context for Infineon's risk management framework and the corporate risk management (CRM) function, we have provided some brief background material on these various issues.

Historical Context

Prior to its spin off from Siemens AG in 1999, Infineon was known as the Siemens Semiconductor Group. As such, Infineon has been actively involved in the development, manufacture, and marketing of semiconductors since 1952. In the 1960s, Siemens Semiconductor Group pioneered the development of integrated circuits (ICs) for use in consumer products.

Infineon has experienced compound annual revenue growth of approximately 28 percent over its last six financial years. It has risen from being the 15th largest supplier of semiconductors and systems worldwide to the eighth largest in 1999.

Infineon's Objectives

Infineon's primary business objectives are to:

- Capitalize on its leadership in ICs in fast-growing areas served by its different divisions.
- Focus on increasing market penetration with major international customers.
- Utilize its intellectual property portfolio to develop ICs tailored to meet customers' specific needs.
- Share risk and expand its access to leading edge technology through long-term strategic partnerships with other leading industry participants.
- Enhance its position as an innovation and technology leader by continuing to invest in research and development (R&D).
- Exploit and, as appropriate, expand its world-class manufacturing capabilities.
- Attract and retain senior management and other highly qualified personnel, in particular R&D personnel, by fostering employee ownership through employee share ownership and share option plans.

Joint Ventures and Alliances

Infineon has a number of alliances and joint ventures with other parties. These help to improve the corporate risk profile because:

- They create new opportunities but also limit risk through sharing of technology and manpower.

- They help to share the volatility inherent in the semiconductor market.
- They enable exchange and extension of resources.

Primary Drivers of ERM at Infineon

As with several of the other case study organizations profiled in this publication, especially those outside the U.S., corporate governance initiatives have been a leading driver of ERM at Infineon. Specifically, KonTraG, the German corporate governance regime, has been a primary influencing factor (see Table 0.1 and http://www.bmj.bund.de/misc/e_kont.htm for further information).

Another primary driver has been senior management's desire to go further than simple compliance with KonTraG, by making Infineon's risk management system meaningful and value adding to the organization. This is probably best described by the following statement from Infineon's 20-F Report: "Beyond the scope of the legal requirement, our risk management system is intended to enhance our company's value by pursuing an opportunity-oriented decision-making strategy in consideration of the respective risks."

Infineon's Forecasting Process

Each Infineon business division produces a monthly update of its rolling forecast of results for the next eight quarters. Monthly forecasting is critical for Infineon because:

- Stock market analysts and the SEC want to see that level of transparency in the business on a quarterly basis.
- Without the forecasting, rapid response to market developments would be more difficult.
- Control options need to be identified early on.
- Production cycles can be very short for some products.
- Massive investment is required on manufacturing facilities as well as R&D. Most semi-conductor companies are cash-negative because of these demands.

Business divisions complete a risk/opportunity report as an attachment to their monthly forecast. A copy of the form used is shown in Figure 8.1. Infineon defines risk as: *the threats and opportunities that fall outside the normal forecasting process and can therefore produce variation from forecast results.* The threshold for risk to be reported is an EBIT value in excess of Euro 25 million, after allowing for risk improvement measures. However, regardless of the threshold, business units must report their top five risks/opportunities.

Figure 8.1
Infineon Technologies -- Monthly Risk Report Format

CORPORATE RISK MANAGEMENT   RISK/OPPORTUNITY REPORT BUSINESS GROUPS

Business Group:
Period: mm/yy

No.	Risks/Opport unities No. Category	Cross Ref.	Risks	Period	Month of Identific.	Measures		Previous month				Actual Month mm/yy			
								Impact on EBIT	Prob-ability	Risks/ Opportunities in FC. ytd.	Impl. Status	Impact on EBIT	Prob-ability	R/O in FC. ytd	Impl. Status
(1)	(2)	(3)	(4)	(5)	(6)	(7)	(8)	(9)	(10)	(11)	(12)	(13)	(14)	(15)	(16)
1															
2															
3															
4															
5															
			Opportunities												
1															
2															
3															
4															

Analysis and Comments

1
2
3
4
5

Linking the risk report to the monthly forecasting and business monitoring processes was seen as essential, because it would help management to understand why a forecast might prove to be under or overstated, and to what extent. Completing the form forces each business to consider the factors that could cause variation in their forecast. This means that if the forecast is not met, it should be because of a risk that has been previously identified.

Through the risk/opportunity report, the quality of forecasting has improved. For example:

- Business managers have become better accustomed to looking at forecasting horizons.
- Greater consistency in forecasting prices is now being seen. This should in turn lead to improved machinery utilization.
- Senior management has become more attuned to looking at and understanding the risks identified.
- Less blame is attached to managers for missing a forecast, as long as the risk factor had been previously identified on the monthly risk report.

Corporate Risk Management (CRM) Mission

The mission defined for Infineon's Corporate Risk Management (CRM) function is tied back to the business objectives, corporate governance guidelines, and forecasting process discussed above. The overall intention is not to avoid risks, but to enhance the ability of the organization to manage its risk exposures. Specifically, the CRM mission is to:

- Satisfy KonTraG requirements.
- Produce an opportunity-oriented risk decision-making process.
- Identify and measure threats to Infineon's:
    - Technological capabilities.
    - Earnings and cash capacity.
    - Assets.
    - Reputation.
    - Stakeholder confidence.
- Focus management action on priority risk areas.

The senior director of CRM reports to Infineon's CFO, although he also regularly discusses risk report matters with the chief operating office (COO). Success or failure of the CRM function is assessed through feedback from business groups and other staff functions.

Other specialist departments involved in different aspects of managing risk include property protection, environmental protection, health and safety, legal, patent, contract management, human resources, and corporate audit. Each of these also provides CRM with a risk report.

The specific role of corporate audit is to provide an independent assurance of the risk management system. Corporate audit included risk management within its area of responsibility until February 2000, but Infineon's senior management has accepted that it does not belong there. The role of corporate audit is to:

- Conduct independent auditing reports.
- Review process effectiveness to see whether the processes work.

Auditing is not holistic in scope, whereas the job of risk management is to look at missed opportunities and potential threats within the core processes of the organization.

Infineon's ERM Process

The current ERM framework used by CRM was originally created within Siemens but adapted by Infineon through, for instance, applying it to a monthly (rather than quarterly as at Siemens) forecasting process, and requiring risk reports from staff functions as well. An underlying principle of Infineon's ERM process is that responsibility for identifying, evaluating, and handling risks should be vested in the business divisions and with those accountable for implementing individual core processes.

The ERM process used at Infineon is as follows:

1. Risk and Opportunity Identification: this is accomplished by having senior management from the business divisions either complete a questionnaire or participate in a 1.5-day workshop facilitated by CRM.
2. Risk and Opportunity Evaluation: this involves developing an assessment of the probability and financial impact for each of the risks and opportunities identified.
3. Risk Handling: this means putting in risk reduction measures or opportunity enhancements.
4. Risk Reporting: this is achieved internally through the risk/opportunity reports described previously. Reporting on risk to outside parties is limited to the 20-F report. An example of key sources of risk at Infineon, as communicated to shareholders in the 20-F report, is given in Table 8.1.

Table 8.1. Key Sources of Risk at Infineon*	
■ Periodic turndowns	■ Changes in exchange rates
■ Intense competition	■ Environmental laws and regulations
■ Industry over-capacity	■ Reductions in the amount of government subsidies and grants
■ Rapid technological change and evolving standards	■ Product liability or warranty claims
■ Proprietary intellectual property	■ Inability to successfully integrate acquisitions
■ Matching production capacity to demand	■ Rights to key intellectual property arrangements
■ Problems with manufacturing	■ Siemens may use the intellectual property to which it retained rights, although transferred to Infineon
■ Limited number of suppliers	■ Siemens might exercise partial control over some of Infineon's intellectual property rights
■ Access to capital	■ Difficulties in operating as an independent company
■ Attracting and retaining qualified personnel	■ Financial information may not be representative of Infineon's results
■ The Siemens Group is Infineon's largest customer	■ Siemens may exert control over Infineon's business
■ Strategic partners	■ The Siemens Group companies may have conflicts of interest that affect Infineon's ongoing business arrangements with them
■ Volatility in different parts of the world	■ Sales of a substantial number of shares

* The 20-F report contains further detail for each item (see http://www.infineon.com).

Aggregation

Infineon has five business groups, one sales group, which is itself a collation of regional sales forecasts, and two "clusters" or factories, of which there are 19 in all.

The CRM department receives a total of eight risk/opportunity reports each month (one for each business group, one for the sales group, one report for the front-end factories, and one for the back-end factories). CRM then reviews the reports received, discusses with and challenges each entity on whether the handling measures are being followed up, and produces an overall group version of the risk report after eliminating double counting.

Guidelines

Principles and guidelines are defined in detail and communicated for every individual risk category. The risk categories adopted by CRM are:

- Business risk.
- Operational management risk, subdivided into:
  - Technical and product development.
  - Manufacturing and logistics.
  - Strategy, marketing, and sales.
  - Organization and management.
- Financial risk.
- IT risk.
- Purchasing risk.
- Legal and compliance risk.
- Human resource risk.

Culture and Other Challenges

Culture remains one of the biggest challenges to institutionalizing a risk reporting process. Developing an understanding of what "risk" means among management is also a major issue; many still think of it only in terms of hazards, or catastrophes, or safety/security, etc. Another challenge has been persuading the business divisions to release their senior managers to participate in the 1.5-day risk identification workshop. Finally, as in many other organizations, it is a challenge to determine at what point a risk management process needs to be installed in the core processes of the organization and then ensure that the process is effectively installed.

The Future

Some changes to the CRM processes anticipated in the future will be:

- Moving to Web-based applications. This will help each business to review not only what it should produce for each month's risk report, but also its past reports. It will also help with communication across disciplines and with the exchange of experiences.
- Ensuring that aggregation is done in a sound fashion so that linkages to risk and effects on other parts of the organization are recognized.
- Introducing new analytical tools to help managers better understand and manage their own risks. For instance, simulation packages may be made available to help managers understand probability and model the alternative ranges of results their businesses could achieve.

CHAPTER 9
HOLCIM LTD.

Overview

The Holcim case provides readers with a step-by-step approach to implementing ERM within the organization. Specifically, process steps, organizational issues, and linkages to the business planning process are provided as examples other organizations may be able to follow as they consider an ERM process.

Holcim Ltd.

(Formerly named Holderbank Financiere Glarus AG)

Headquarters: Jona, Switzerland
Primary Industry: Construction – Raw Materials
Internet: http://www.holderbank.com

2000 Data:
Annual Sales ($Mil): 8,291
Annual Assets ($Mil): 15,237
Number of Employees: 44,316

Description: Holcim is one of the world's leading suppliers of cement, aggregates, and concrete. From origins in Switzerland, the group has grown into a global player with strong market presence in over 70 countries on all continents. More than 40,000 highly skilled employees contribute to the continuing success of "Holderbank" using modern technology that strengthens cost leadership and enhances environmental efficiency." (Source: www.holderbank.com)

Background to ERM at Holcim

Similar to other case study organizations profiled in this publication, Holcim, formerly known as Holderbank Financiere Glarus AG (Holderbank), has adapted its approach to ERM to fit its unique business, structure, and organizational culture. For example, as a group it has these features:

- Global business in cement, concrete, and aggregates (number two worldwide).

- Very dispersed geographically and highly decentralized, operating with four official languages (English, French, Spanish, and German).
- Dr. h.c. Schmidheiny, chairman and chief executive, is also the majority shareholder.
- The group is organized around its group companies, of which there are about 70. There is one group company per country ranging in size from 50 to 2,500 people. The largest is in the U.S., where the group company is a U.S. $1.3 billion business and number one in its field.
- Holcim has only a few mandatory standards that have to be applied uniformly across the group (e.g., International Accounting Standards).
- There are a number of other "corporate programs" adopted by the executive committee and spread by encouragement of best practices. Examples of these include logistics, maintenance, implementation of SAP, engineering, asset reduction, etc.

A number of internal and external challenges have encouraged Holcim to develop its own ERM process — known as Business Risk Management (BRM). Key drivers have been:

- A new corporate governance regime for Swiss companies demanding greater responsibility of board directors (largely non-executives) as well as liability for scrutinizing and challenging the decisions of executive management.
- Increased competition.
- Increasing concentration of customers.
- A gradual move away from Holcim's decentralized style of management toward more of a group structure.
- The desire to avoid or mitigate the sort of high-profile problems that have afflicted multinational corporations, such as the Leeson/Barings affair.

Figure 9.1, taken from an internal Holcim presentation, as are all other slides included in this case study, illustrates the link between some of these "issues" and the "solution," firm-wide business risk and opportunity management.

BRM came into existence approximately two years ago and was one of the first corporate management tools required within all group companies. At the outset no directly quantifiable financial benefit was demanded from the BRM process. However, the Holcim executive committee is convinced that BRM — once fully implemented — will deliver the following soft and hard benefits:

- Increased risk awareness and sensitivity in the entire group.
- Improved communication both horizontally and vertically.
- Better and more proactive management of change.

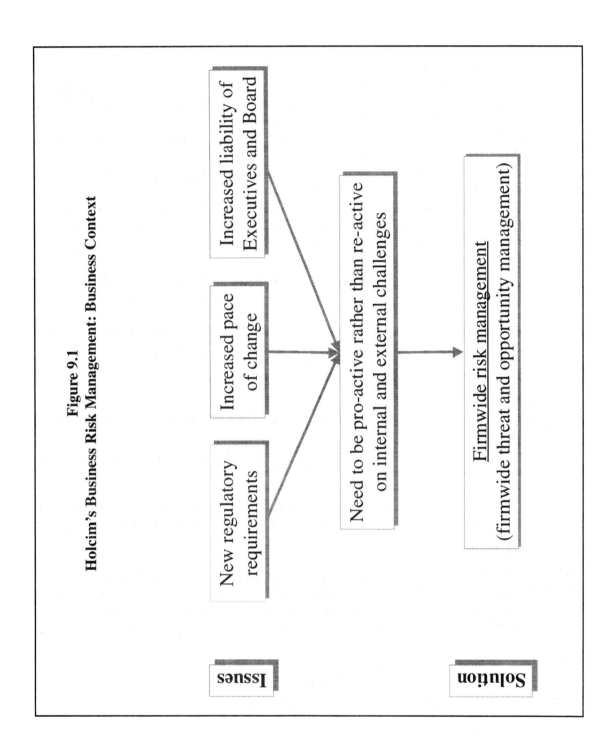

Figure 9.1
Holcim's Business Risk Management: Business Context

- Enhanced reputation.
- More robust business plans together with improved business process guidance.
- Reduced insurance costs as well as eventually lower capital costs.

The BRM Process

The BRM process focuses on strategic risks and is strongly linked with the group companies' business planning process. Each group company discusses with the responsible member of the group executive committee its particular risk exposure and especially the possible impact of the key risks on their business plan. For each key risk, risk management strategies are defined either by avoiding, retaining, reducing, transferring, or exploiting the risk. The actions related to the chosen strategy are incorporated into the business plan.

Figure 9.5 illustrates the closeness of the link between BRM and the business planning process steps.

In order to ensure leadership from the top, either the CEO or a delegated member of each group company executive committee owns and is committed to the BRM process. In addition, each Holcim group company nominates a risk champion who is ideally also responsible for the business plan or for internal audit (IA) in that company. It is the risk champion's task to implement and maintain the BRM process at the local group company with the support of the BRM core team. This BRM core team currently has three members, including a head who reports directly to the group chairman. The BRM core team develops, implements, and oversees the BRM process.

Figure 9.2 illustrates both how BRM is linked to corporate strategy and its position in the control cycle.

A major task for the BRM core team at the beginning of the BRM journey was to identify a set of approximately 40 generic risks for each of Holcim's business segments. This was honed down from a longer list of 200 risks. The idea of the Holcim generic risk categories (Figure 9.3) is to define risks in broad terms, thus helping to define and maintain a common risk language and a common understanding of the risks. The generic risk categories are clarified further by detailed definitions and checklists for the typical industry-specific sources of the respective risks.

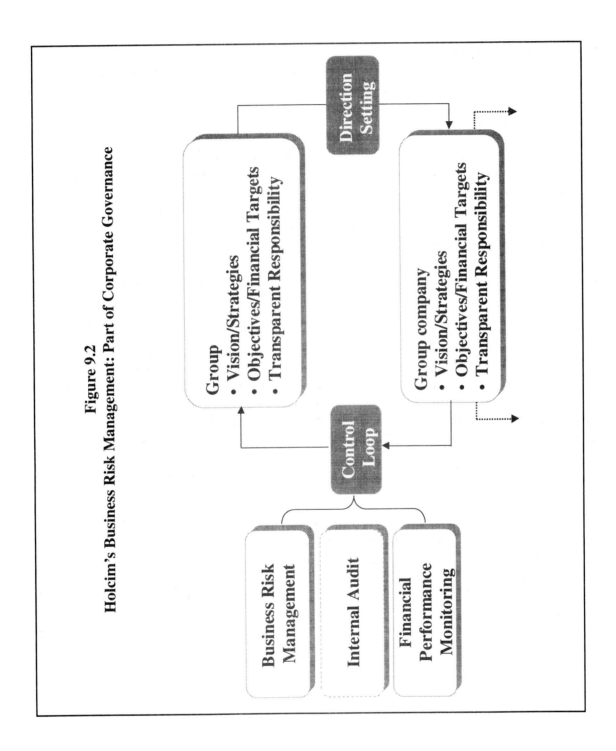

Figure 9.2
Holcim's Business Risk Management: Part of Corporate Governance

Figure 9.3
Risk Model = Holcim's Generic Risk Categories

1. Business Environment Risks

1.1 Industry & Market

1.1.1 Competitor Actions
1.1.2 Economic Influences
1.1.3 Currency
1.1.4 Interest Rates

1.2 External Stakeholders

1.2.1 Shareholder Relations
1.2.2 Government/Public Influences
1.2.3 Capital Availability
1.2.4 Reputation

1.3 Laws & Regulations

1.3.1 Compliance
1.3.2 Future Regulations

1.4 Catastrophic Events

1.4.1 Catastrophe

2. Business Process Risks

2.1 Value Chain

2.1.1 Resource Availability
2.1.2 Capacity
2.1.3 Efficiency/Productiv.
2.1.4 Service/Prod. Quality
2.1.5 Environmental
2.1.6 Logistics
2.1.7 Business Interruption
2.1.8 Selling/Pricing
2.1.9 Outsourcing
2.1.10 Contracts
2.1.11 CAPEX Projects
2.1.12 Procurement

2.2 Information Management

2.2.1 IT Security
2.2.2 Information Relevance
2.2.3 IT Infrastructure

2.3 Planning & Monitoring

2.3.1 Business Plan
2.3.2 Measurem./Monitoring
2.3.3 Business Portfolio

2.4 Finance

2.4.1 Credit Default
2.4.2 Financial Instruments
2.4.3 Liquidity/Cash Flow
2.4.4 Asset Protection
2.4.5 Taxation
2.4.6 Pension Funding
2.4.7 Financial Reporting
2.4.8 Budget & Planning

2.5 People

2.5.1 Hiring/Retaining
2.5.2 Empowerment
2.5.3 Fraud & Corruption
2.5.4 Health & Safety
2.5.5 Social Security
2.5.6 Personal Security

Applying the BRM process in each group company involves the following six steps:

Step 1: Is a 1.5 day workshop facilitated by the BRM core team where group company executives are tasked with ranking the relative position of each of the 40 generic risks for their company in a risk map, in terms of probability and significance (impact). A time scale of three to five years in alignment with the business plan period sets the timing for determining the likelihood and the significance of a business risk. To the extent possible, the significance is estimated in terms of its potential financial consequence. Color-coding indicates high impact/high probability (red), low impact/low probability (green), and in between (yellow). Figure 9.4 provides an illustrative example of how the generic risks are mapped and color-coded onto the significance/likelihood matrix, the so-called actual risk map.

Step 2: Looks in more detail at the key risks shown in the red quartile of the risk map. The goal of this step is to break down the risks into their influencing factors, which are named risk drivers. Mind-mapping is used to show the connections between the individual drivers and the risk. Each key risk is then assigned to the executive-level manager in the best position to oversee and manage the risk.

Step 3: Is a quantification process, which analyzes the key risk drivers for "red" risks in terms of "significance" (the threshold is five percent of EBIT) on planned net profit over the next five years (business plan period). Upside as well as downside potential is considered.

Step 4: Is where the executives agree on the desired risk profile, achievable via the actions identified by the management. Once possible risk management alternatives have been identified and evaluated, the executives are in a position to choose the set of risk mitigation actions that best fulfil the strategic goals set by the management. The outcome of this step is the target risk map, which represents the desired and attainable position of each individual risk, together with an action plan consisting of risk mitigating actions necessary to achieve the target risk map.

Step 5: Involves integration into the business planning process. In order to ensure sustainability as well as success, the actions defined in step 4 have to be integrated in the business plan. Figure 9.5 provides a graphic illustration of how BRM is linked and integrated into Holcim's business planning process.

Step 6: Includes monitoring and reporting. The BRM process implemented in the Holcim Group companies is not a one-off exercise but rather an ongoing management process with annual updates. The companies must evaluate whether progress in managing the risk and achieving the desired target risk map has actually been made.

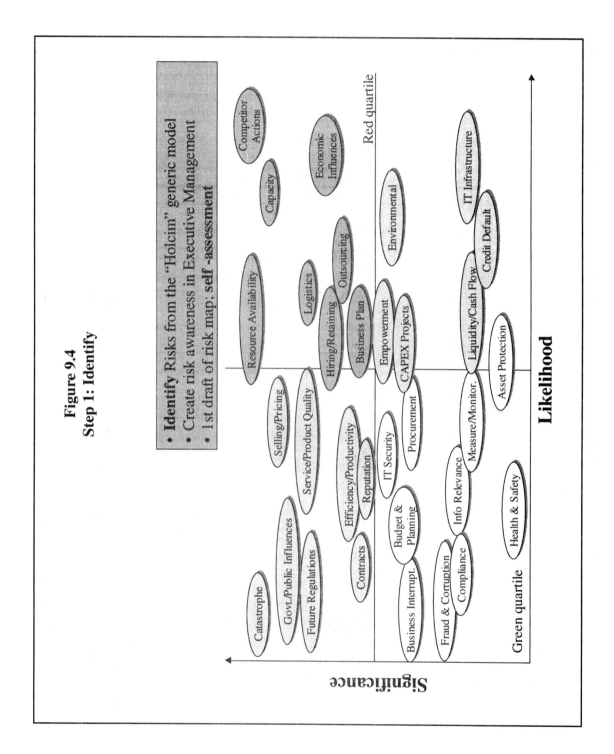

Figure 9.4
Step 1: Identify

- **Identify Risks from the "Holcim" generic model**
- Create risk awareness in Executive Management
- 1st draft of risk map; **self -assessment**

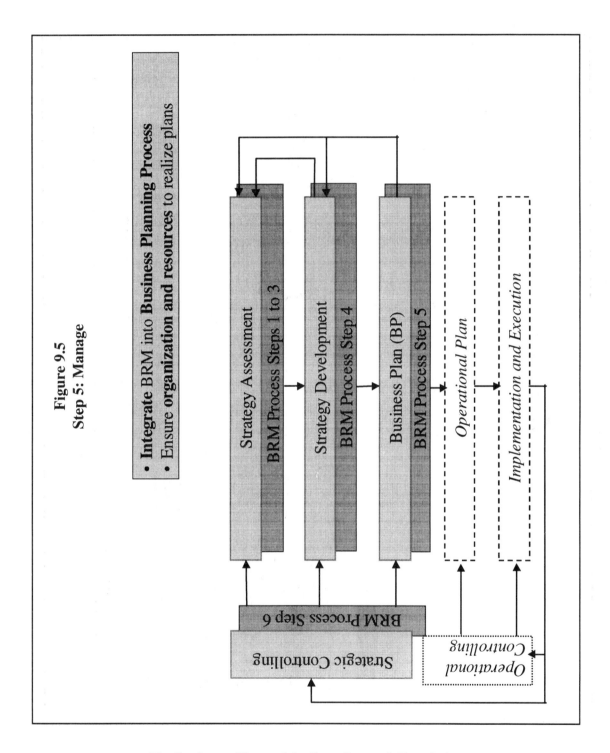

Figure 9.5
Step 5: Manage

Four key words are used by Holcim to describe its BRM process:

- Comprehensive (internal & external challenges).
- Proactive (risk awareness throughout the organization; anticipation of future developments).
- Systematic (systematic and integrated approach, continuous process).
- Multipliable (common language and process in all group companies).

In order to guarantee sustainability as well as quality of process and result in each group company, minimum requirements (including a mandatory compliance report) for the annual update of the BRM process have been put in place.

IT Support

The elaborated risk documents for each group company are held in a series of Lotus Notes databases created specifically for Holcim. Because of the confidentiality of the companies' risk information, significant work went into addressing security issues and limiting access to each group company's data. The selected concept/structure of the database ensures an easy distribution of generic and normative information on the one hand as well as a secure storage source for the critical local risk documents on the other hand. A link between group companies and the BRM core team enables the desired knowledge sharing while still providing strict confidentiality. With its comprehensive store of information, the database is also used as a reporting tool.

Aggregation of Risks

The BRM core team is currently in the process of elaborating the first aggregated risk report for the most important business segment (cement) on a group level. The basis of this report are the individual risk documents — mainly the risk map and the risk driver mind maps — of all group companies, as well as the risk documents prepared by the group executive committee. It is the goal of the report to define critical business areas where corporate efforts are required as well as to align the view of the group companies and the group executive management with regard to the threats and opportunities each company faces.

Role of Internal Audit

Until the beginning of this year Holcim had no group-level IA function. Approximately half of the group companies had their own IA function. Last year the situation was evaluated in light of corporate governance requirements for each of the individual group companies as well as of the group. For risks, which are to be considered as relevant, but not key as per the BRM process, the basic outline for a respective IA framework has been defined.

Figure 9.6 illustrates how BRM and IA will work together on related but distinct aspects of risk management. The role of IA at the group level is not that of a policeman, but to ensure compliance reporting by means of a self-assessment questionnaire. The development of the audit approach is part of the BRM head's responsibilities.

Recommendations for BRM Implementation

Dos

- Prepare ground for implementation through piloting, use feedback of pilots as selling proposition.
- Define common risk model and language before starting (in order to avoid reinventing the wheel).
- Use efficient tools in the implementation process.
- Prepare organization: nominate people responsible for BRM on group company level (risk champion and one member of group company executive committee, usually CEO).

Don'ts

- Don't do it without top management commitment.
- Don't use it as a standalone tool. "Sell" it as a "normal" management tool and integrate it in other management procedures/tools (e.g., business plan).

Challenges/Recommendations

- Sustainability in using the tool and in applying it as normal management process.
- Financial Consolidation: only feasible for financial data/risk.
- If not doing it you will be challenged sooner or later by financial community (corporate governance) and you will have to pay an additional premium for capital.

Figure 9.6
Business Risk Management: Part of Corporate Governance

	Business risks			Financial performance monitoring risks
	Strategic risks	Major one-off risks	Operational risks	
	Business Risk Management		Internal Audit	
Typical responsibility for **defining a mandatory process**	BRM	BRM / *Internal Audit*	Internal Audit *BRM*	Internal Audit / *External Audit*
Typical responsibility for **monitoring the adherence to the mandatory process**				

The Institute of Internal Auditors Research Foundation

CHAPTER 10
WAL-MART STORES, INC.

Overview

The Wal-Mart case provides readers with an overview of an evolution toward enterprise risk management (ERM) within a retail environment. The case shows how Wal-Mart links ERM with the business vision and objectives. It also demonstrates a unique approach to implementing ERM through facilitative workshops. The case concludes with some insights about the role of organizational culture and lessons learned.

Wal-Mart Stores, Inc.

Headquarters: Bentonville, Arkansas, USA
Primary Industry: Retail
Internet: http://www.walmart.com

2000 Data:
Annual Sales ($Mil): 191,329
Annual Assets ($Mil): 78,130
Number of Employees: 1,244,000

Description: "Wal-Mart Stores, Inc. principally is engaged in the operation of mass merchandising stores, which serve customers primarily through the operation of three divisions. The Wal-Mart Stores division includes the Company's discount stores and Supercenters in the United States. The SAM'S Club division includes the warehouse membership clubs in the United States. The International division includes all operations in Argentina, Brazil, Canada, China, Germany, Korea, Mexico, Puerto Rico, and the United Kingdom." (Source: Market Guide business description as found on www.onesource.com.)

Background of ERM at Wal-Mart

Wal-Mart Stores, Inc. (Wal-Mart) began looking at an ERM approach in late 1998 - early 1999. There were a number of factors motivating their interest in ERM, including the emergence of new risks associated with their rapid growth and global expansion. There was a general feeling that they had done quite well in executing their strategic growth plans and that they had the ability to react tactically to challenges in an effective way. However, they believed that they could manage the key risks to their business in a more proactive and formalized way.

When Wal-Mart compared the traditional approach to risk management with the concept of ERM, they saw several distinct advantages. Under a traditional risk management framework, risk is generally treated in "silos" — either by function (i.e., merchandising, operations, payroll, logistics, legal) or by risk specialty. The problem with the silo approach is that it is vertical in focus and presents only a limited view of complex problems. Another limitation is that information is not as easily shared across functions and risks are prioritized independently. The managers at Wal-Mart felt that when it comes to the bottom line, the silo approach tends to lead to higher risk management costs in the long run.

On the other hand, an ERM framework takes a cross-functional approach that is both horizontal and vertical in focus. Wal-Mart felt that ERM could provide a more comprehensive view of risks and yield more integrated solutions. An ERM framework could also help facilitate the exchange of information across functions and coordinate the prioritization of risks. In this way, they could identify and exploit the various risk interrelationships — and in the end have a more cost-effective risk management strategy. The promise of ERM seemed superior to the traditional framework.

Wal-Mart's ERM Framework

At the base of Wal-Mart's ERM framework is its ERM Mission stating that:

- Risks are understood, measured, and controlled.
- Business objectives are achieved through:
  - Anticipation of critical events, and
  - Rapid implementation of optimal decisions.

For Wal-Mart, risk is defined as "*Anything that prevents you from achieving your business objectives.*" With that definition in mind, ERM interlocks with both crisis management and strategic planning. When viewed on a timeline, ERM occupies the middle ground between these two functions (see Figure 10.1). Crisis management deals with urgent issues today whereas ERM looks out 12 to 18 months and strategic planning looks down the road three to five years. This is all done within the context of Wal-Mart's core business processes (see Figure 10.2).

The Institute of Internal Auditors Research Foundation

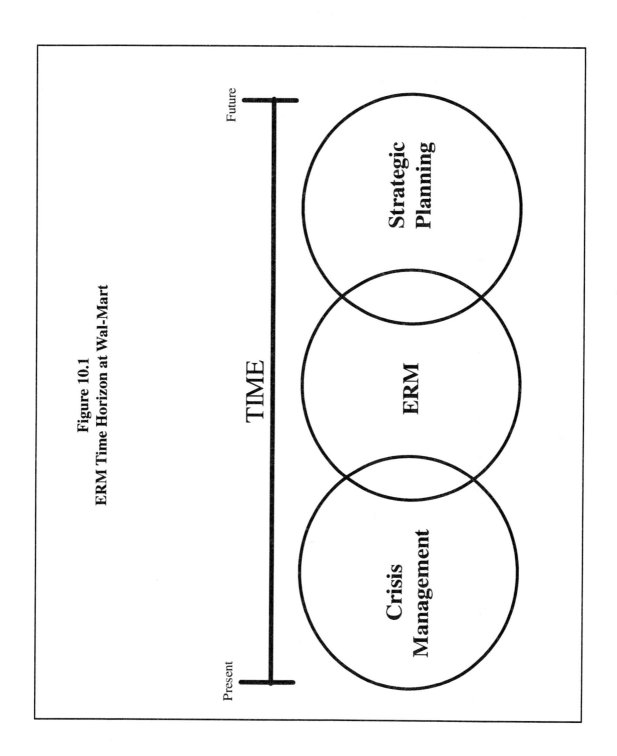

Figure 10.1
ERM Time Horizon at Wal-Mart

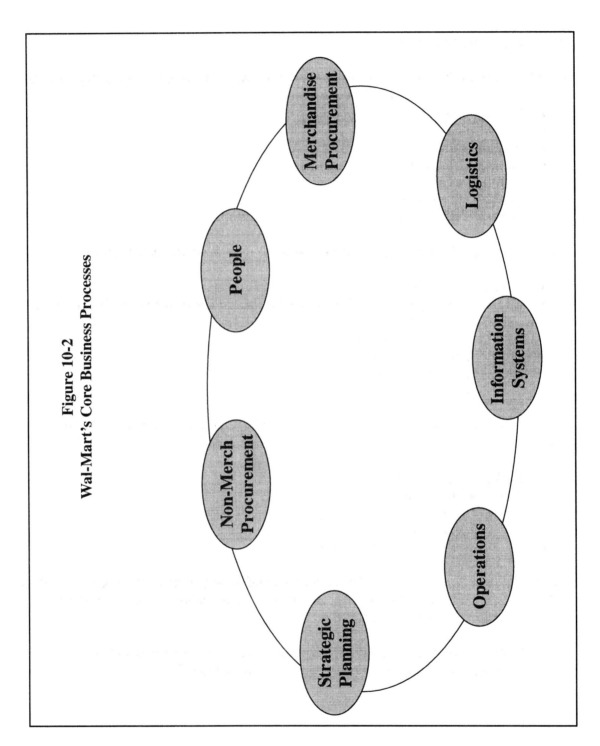

Figure 10-2
Wal-Mart's Core Business Processes

The Institute of Internal Auditors Research Foundation

Wal-Mart's ERM Process

Wal-Mart's overall ERM process has evolved over the last two years and its seven steps include:

- Business vision.
- Business objective.
- Risk framework.
- Identify risk universe.
- Risk workshop.
- Control and action workshop.
- Monitor, evaluate, manage.

For example, the following represents the business vision of one of its operating units:

- To be market share leader;
- To be lowest cost provider of goods and services to our customers, while maximizing shareholder value; and
- To live our three basic beliefs:
  - Respect for the Individual.
  - Service to our Customer.
  - Strive for Excellence.

The corresponding business objectives flowing from this vision are represented in the following ideas:

- Expansion opportunities.
- Build distribution network.
- Improve customer service.
- Retention of associates.
- Associate training and development.

Once the business vision and objectives have been clarified and recorded, the risk framework is outlined. The risk framework provides a standard and consistent frame of reference and organizes risks into the following two primary categories:

- External risks (e.g., legal/regulatory, political issues, business environment).
- Internal risks (e.g., strategic, operational, financial, integrity).

Wal-Mart then sets about to identify its risk universe within the context of the risk framework described above. To achieve this, key decision-makers across the various functions are surveyed and asked to identify six of the greatest risks to Wal-Mart's business objectives. The ERM Committee then compiles the data into a risk matrix (usually 50 risks) and merges the responses into 20 to 35 risk categories. This committee is composed of several individuals from various functions throughout Wal-Mart and is championed by the vice president of internal auditing and co-chaired by the senior director of risk management. After the ERM Committee has sifted through the survey data and categorized the information appropriately, the information is provided to the risk workshop participants.

Similar to the ERM Committee, Wal-Mart's risk workshops strive to achieve cross-functional representation. The workshops involve 15 to 20 people, including one or two facilitators and one or two recorders. An ERM facilitator coordinates and conducts each workshop and helps participants reach common understanding and definitions of the risks identified during the survey described above. After discussion, the participants vote anonymously on the probability (likelihood) and impact (severity) of each risk, net of controls. Probability and impact are measured on a scale of 1 to 10 (i.e., low/medium/high scale). If the standard deviation of responses around a single risk is ≥ 3, then there is an additional discussion about the risk and a revote. The ultimate goal of the risk workshop is to produce a two-dimensional risk map (probability and impact).

The next step in Wal-Mart's ERM process is to conduct control and action planning workshops. These meetings are designed to evaluate the high priority risks that emerged from the risk workshops in terms of potential exposure, existing controls, and control deficiencies. The control and action planning workshops are smaller in size than the risk workshops, comprising approximately eight to 12 individuals. The participants of this workshop are also cross-functional and may or may not be the same individuals who participated in the risk workshop. The ultimate purpose of the control and action-planning workshop is to develop an action plan and assign responsibility.

The final step in the ERM process is to monitor, evaluate, and manage the action plans created in the previous step. This involves setting specific measurements and a timeline (a scorecard), monitoring the progress, and addressing any gaps that may arise. The results are reported quarterly.

The results for Wal-Mart of the ERM process outlined above are threefold. First, the risk universe is identified; second, specific action plans are established and monitored; and third, the information is used to create a global risk map.

Status of Wal-Mart's ERM Process

Since deciding on the facilitative workshop approach described above in May 2000, Wal-Mart completed a pilot program for all of its Canadian operations in the fall of 2000. As of February 2001, they had conducted workshops in 60 percent of the operations within each of their three divisions. They hope to repeat this process each year and they would like to see the workshops eventually become self-sustaining at the divisional levels. On average, participants have rated the ERM process "4.3 out of 5."

Cultural/Organizational Issues that Help Facilitate the ERM Process at Wal-Mart

The organizational culture established by Wal-Mart's founder, Sam Walton, has been an asset as Wal-Mart has embarked on ERM. For example, managers have traditionally looked for cross-functional solutions to their problems, rather than through a silo approach. They also have an open-minded culture to change and the belief that you "need to set your ego aside." As described earlier, Wal-Mart's three values (Respect for the Individual, Service to our Customer, and Strive for Excellence) are also part of the organizational culture that seems to have helped facilitate the implementation of ERM. Given this culture, they have not discussed the need for a chief risk officer position and believe they may not need such a position (the CFO is the CRO).

In Canada, ERM buy-in was achieved through the influence of the CEO of international, who was predisposed to the concept. In the U.S., it was introduced not as ERM, but as an enhancement to the regular internal auditing risk assessment process.

Future Plans

While Wal-Mart has taken significant strides in the implementation of their ERM framework, there is still work to be done. They expect the risks to their business will evolve as they experience continued growth, especially internationally. A few representative plans for the future include:

- Get buy-in from the executive committee, audit committee, and eventually the full board.
- Institutionalize the ERM process. This could be impeded if the process becomes too bureaucratic or if it is not seen as adding value. ERM has to help Wal-Mart's key decision makers reach their business objectives.
- Utilize the ERM process to complement strategic planning for the international segment (i.e., ERM will be conducted in countries where strategic planning is not scheduled to occur within the same year).

The Institute of Internal Auditors Research Foundation

Recommendations/Lessons Learned

- Benchmark successful organizations.
- Decide/agree on definition of ERM and on what you want to accomplish.
- Don't introduce ERM as something new; introduce it as an enhancement to something that's already entrenched.
- Customize the process for your unique business environment and requirements.
- Involve representatives from strategic planning.
- Use outside consultants to train an internal team of workshop facilitators. The training should include mock workshops and facilitators should be given "timeouts" to receive feedback.
- Conduct the facilitative workshops off-site.
- Don't try to force the process on anyone.
- Sell it as bits and pieces — the risk assessment and the risk management. The pilot program was very helpful.

PART III:
SUMMARY AND CONCLUSIONS

The Current State of ERM

Quite a number of organizations — large and small, across varied industries — are undertaking ERM. Their motivations range from external pressure (e.g., corporate governance guidelines, regulations, institutional investor concerns) to sound business practice to competitive advantage. Many have developed new tools and metrics. Some have successfully integrated ERM with other processes such as internal auditing and strategic planning. None acknowledge having completed the process. The "ERM movement" is still in its early years, but clearly already has its very strong adherents.

Implementing ERM

It is fair to say that no two organizations are taking the same route to ERM. Most are proceeding incrementally. Some are beginning by layering additional sources of risk, one at a time, into their existing processes for assessment, mitigation, etc. Some are embracing all sources of risk at the outset, but are tackling the processes one at a time, with most starting with risk assessment. Others are taking on all risk sources and all processes, but on a small, manageable subset of their operations as a "pilot project." Most all are seeking "early wins" that will help build momentum and promote further development toward their ideal ERM process.

Issues to Consider

As organizations move forward with ERM they need to consider a number of items:

- Which conceptual model of ERM will be used and what adaptations will be necessary to meet the organization's needs?
- How will it be rolled out within the organization, e.g., geographically, by organizational unit, key functions?
- How "deep" is senior management's support?
- What tools and metrics should be employed?
- Will ERM be used as a management information tool or as a performance driver?
- Should ERM be linked to compensation and incentive design?
- How should ERM be communicated to stakeholders, if at all?

Success Factors

As our research and case studies demonstrate, there are a number of key success factors for the successful implementation of an ERM program (see Figure III.1).

Obtaining key management support is absolutely crucial. As the survey data indicates, there are significant cultural and organizational barriers to implementing ERM. Obtaining senior management support and making ERM a senior management agenda item is vital to overcoming some of these barriers.

Implementing ERM cannot be a done on a part-time basis. Successful implementation models found in the cases each had a dedicated group of staff to drive ERM implementation and to continue to push it in its operational phase.

Moreover, for a number of organizations, ERM is rolled out in modular form rather than across the entire enterprise. This modular concept can be either within an organizational unit or across key functions such as finance/treasury. Obviously the size and complexity of the organization will determine the best rollout strategy.

Given the time and effort to deploy a comprehensive ERM program across the entire organization, providing justification in the form of a business case is critical.

In fact these success factors are not mutually exclusive but reinforcing. Providing a business case can help gain top management support. A modular rollout can facilitate the management of some of the cultural issues and create "wins" for the ERM team.

The Future of ERM

It seems clear that ERM is more than another management fad or buzzword of the moment, and more than an academic theory. Organizations with a reputation for good management are often those doing ERM before their peers. We believe ERM will become an integral part of the management process for organizations of the 21st century. It will influence how organizations are structured, with some appointing a chief risk officer that reports to the CEO or board of directors. It will influence how strategic planning is done. And it will certainly influence how internal auditing is performed.

Figure III.1
ERM Implementation Key Success Factors

- Having strong and visible support from senior management (e.g., CEO, CFO, CRO);

- Having a dedicated group of cross-functional staff to drive ERM implementation and continue to push it in its operational phase;

- Closely linking ERM to the key strategic and financial objectives of the organization and to the business processes;

- Introducing ERM as an enhancement to already entrenched and well-accepted processes within the organization, rather than as a new, stand-alone process;

- Importing ideas from the outside; and

- Proceeding incrementally and leveraging "early wins."

The Institute of Internal Auditors Research Foundation

APPENDIX I
PROFILE OF SURVEY RESPONDENTS

Type of Organization

Over 130 executives responded to the survey. Public stock organizations make up over half of the sample and private stock organizations account for 16 percent of respondents. The remaining respondents are mutuals, mutual holding organizations, fraternals, governmental entities, non-profits, or others.

Table II.1: Type of Organization	
% of respondents indicating	
Public stock	54%
Private stock	16%
Mutual	2%
Mutual holding organization	2%
Fraternal	1%
Other	17%
No answer	8%

Primary Industries

Nearly 25 percent of the responding organizations have a significant presence in the financial services industry, with half representing insurance and reinsurance organizations and the other half representing various financial services firms (e.g., banks, investment organizations). About 15 percent of the sample are from the energy and mining industry. In addition, 13 percent are major players in the manufacturing sector. Other primary industry groups represented in the sample include the public sector (i.e., governmental entities), telecommunications/IT, technology, retail, healthcare, services, and transportation.

Table II.2: Primary Industries % of respondents indicating	
Energy and mining	15%
Insurance	12%
Other financial services	12%
Manufacturing	13%
Public sector	8%
Telecommunications/IT/Media/ Entertainment	8%
Technology	6%
Healthcare	5%
Retail	5%
Services	4%
Transportation	2%
Other	5%
No answer	5%

Size of Organization

Many of the organizations responding to the survey are among the largest in their respective industries. We measured the size of the responding organizations by their total revenues and assets for their most recently completed fiscal year.

Table II.3: Size of Organization by Total Revenue ($US) % of respondents indicating	
<$100 Million	12%
$100 – $249 Million	8%
$250 - $499 Million	8%
$500 - $999 Million	7%
$1 - $4.9 Billion	31%
$5 - $9.9 Billion	15%
$10 - $24.9 Billion	7%
>$25 Billion	5%
No answer	7%

Table II.4: Size of Organization by Total Assets ($US)

% of respondents indicating

<$250 Million	11%
$250 – $499 Million	7%
$500 - $999 Million	9%
$1 - $4.9 Billion	21%
$5 - $14.9 Billion	18%
$15 - $24.9 Billion	8%
>$25 – $39.9 Billion	8%
>$40 Billion	11%
No answer	7%

Scope of Operations

Table II.5: Scope of Operations

% of respondents indicating

Multinational/global	43%
Presence limited to one country	19%
North America	15%
Presence limited to one territory	8%
Asia/Pacific	2%
Europe	1%
Latin America	0%
Other	4%
No answer	9%

APPENDIX II
COMPLETE SURVEY RESULTS

Complete Survey Results

This section provides the statistical results for each of the survey questions. For some questions, the percentage of respondents selecting each answer is listed. Percentages may not total 100 due to rounding. Also, the percentages for some questions add up to more than 100 because respondents could mark multiple answers.

For other questions (those where they ranked importance), we have provided the weighted average score. The weighted average score was determined by assigning five points to each "high," three points to each "medium," and one point to each "low." All of the points were added and then divided by the total number of respondents. The result was the weighted average score for each response. The higher the weighted average score, the higher the degree of importance. A similar system was used for questions where we asked respondents to rank their top choices.

Status and Definition of ERM in Your Organization

1. How would you characterize the status of your ERM framework? *(Please choose one.)*
    - 11% We have a complete ERM framework currently in place.
    - 38 We have a partial ERM framework currently in place.
    - 20 We do not have an ERM framework now, but we are planning to implement one. *(Please skip to question 3.)*
    - 22 We are investigating the concept of ERM. *(Please skip to question 5.)*
    - 9 We do not have an ERM framework and we are not planning to implement one. *(Please skip to question 6.)*

2. How long have you been operating under this framework? *(Please choose one.)*
    - 31% Less than one year
    - 44 One to two years
    - 12 Three to four years
    - 13 Five years or more

3. Who in the organization is, or will be, primarily responsible for overseeing your ERM activities? (*Please choose one.*)
   7%   Chief Executive Officer (CEO)
   24   Chief Financial Officer (CFO)
   21   Chief Risk Officer (CRO)
   30   Chief Audit Executive
   1   Chief Legal Officer
   16   Other

4. How did you implement, or how do you plan to implement, your ERM activities? (*Please choose all that apply.*)
   42% Globally and holistically
   37   Incrementally, by business segment
   8   Incrementally, by region
   31   Incrementally, by type of risk
   4   Incrementally, other

5. What motivated your ERM activity? (*Please choose all that apply.*)
   25% Compliance with governmental regulation
   10   Compliance with stock exchange regulation
   41   Compliance with corporate governance guidelines
   24   Mandate from Board of Directors
   11   Deregulation
   22   Competitive pressure
   9   Price volatility
   20   Desire for earnings stability
   59   Desire for unifying framework for risk assessment, capital management, asset allocation, etc.
   7   Recent catastrophic event
   19   Other

6. What are the potential barriers to implementing your ERM activities for maximum benefit? *(Please rank the top three issues that affect your organization, with "1" being the greatest barrier.)*

    19% Lack of tools
    36   Organizational "turf" (i.e., internal conflicts over roles and responsibilities)
    46   Lack of formalized processes
    21   Lack of appropriate technology/data
    13   Lack of intellectual capital (i.e., know how)
    55   Organizational culture
    11   Cost
    50   Not perceived as a priority among senior management
    8   Skills/talent
    13   Benefit doesn't justify the effort
    8   Other
    2   Don't know

Organization

7. Please indicate your managerial and/or board committees that regularly deal with risk management and compliance issues. *(Please choose all that apply.)*

    82% Audit committee
    39   Risk management committee
    13   Asset/liability management committee
    22   Investment committee
    8   Compliance/market conduct committee
    47   Executive committee
    12   Other

8. How are your various risk management and compliance committees/activities coordinated overall? *(Please choose all that apply.)*

    90% Report to single executive officer (Please specify which officer.)
        21% Chief Executive Officer (CEO)
        30   Chief Financial Officer (CFO)
        13   Chief Risk Officer (CRO)
        12   Chief Audit Executive
        6   Chief Legal Officer
        8   Other
    22% Activities guided by board mandate
    11% Other
    8% Not coordinated or informal coordination

9. Which of the following roles does the internal auditing function play in assessing and responding to risks that affect the organization? *(Please choose all that apply.)*
   89% Risk-based audits at business level
   32 Participation on ERM committees/working teams
   32 ERM risk assessments
   14 Other
   7 Does not play a role in risk management

10. Please describe other areas of risk management in which internal auditing can or should participate. Representative responses are indicated below:
   - Greater coordination with other risk management activities in the organization to prioritize risk assessment activities.
   - Auditing compliance with financial risk management policies, legal actions/statutes, and regulations.
   - Getting more involved in new ventures and mergers & acquisitions.
   - Letter of representation from business units which states the risks and mitigation tactics for each business unit.
   - Should be directly involved in the governance process and ethical conduct expectations and compliance.
   - Actively participate on technology project steering committees.
   - Assist with the assessment process and determine adequacy of controls once in place.
   - ERM system analysis.
   - Reporting risk profiles to the CEO, top executives, and the board.
   - Operational risk management.
   - Stimulating discussion, debate and awareness among senior management and the board around the topic of risk management.
   - Risk management committee.
   - Helping to keep the risk model current. Aggregating risk among business units to a corporate wide exposure. Updating the audit committee on the success of the program.
   - Possible involvement in risk management from insurance perspective.
   - Internal auditing should conduct workshops to help minimize risk in all areas.
   - Consolidating the risk assessment results into an auditing plan.
   - Developing the ERM framework, methodology, and common risk language.
   - Monitoring of implemented risk mitigation strategies monitoring for compliance with previous recommendations.
   - Credit risk management, financial risk management, business continuity planning, and IT security.

11. Does your company have a Chief Risk Officer (CRO)? *(Please choose one.)*
     24% Yes
     73   No *(Please skip to question 12.)*
     3   No answer

11a. How long has your company had a CRO? *(Please choose one.)*
      40% Less than one year
      23   One to two years
      23   Three to four years
      7   Five years or more

11b. Did the CRO come from an internal position or an external source? *(Please choose one.)*
      71% An internal position (Please specify from which function.)
           11% Risk management
           4   Treasury
           18   Finance
           21   Internal auditing
           18   Other
      29   An external source (Please specify from which source.)
           11% Former CRO in same industry
           4   Former CRO in different industry
      14   Other

11c. To whom does the CRO directly report? *(Please choose one.)*
      35% CEO
      29   CFO
      19   Board
      13   Other

Importance of ERM in Addressing Key Business Issues

12. From the issues listed below, please rank the top five business issues you currently face and the top five you expect to face in the next three years. *(Please use a 1-to-5 scale, with "1" being the most important.)* For each of your top five issues, please indicate whether ERM will help you address that issue.

Business Issues	Importance rank now*	Importance rank three years from now	Will ERM help address?
General			
• Revenue growth	2	2	55%
• Earnings growth	1	1	57%
• Return on capital	4	5	63%
• Earnings consistency	7	3	67%
• Expense control/reduction	3	6	64%
• Product pricing	9	9	68%
• Adequacy of accruals	28 (tie)	30	100%
• Technology costs	5	4	62%
• People costs	6	7	50%
• Treasury risk management	23	23	80%
• Hazard risk management	16	26 (tie)	67%
Internal Financial/Operational			
• Asset/liability management	14 (tie)	15	100%
• Capital management/allocation	11	10	85%
• M&A activity	12	11	74%
• Contingency planning/disaster recovery	24	20 (3 way tie)	100%
• Cash management/liquidity	14 (tie)	18 (tie)	63%
• Financial reporting	28 (tie)	31	100%
• Derivative-based hedging	27	29	100%
• Insurance/reinsurance	30	24	67%

Business Issues	Importance rank now*	Importance rank three years from now	Will ERM help address?
● Financial controls	25 (tie)	17	70%
● Inventory management	20 (tie)	25	40%
● Operating controls	10	13	79%
● Internal financial processes	22	26 (tie)	50%
● Environmental	20 (tie)	20 (3 way tie)	67%
● Research/intellectual property	31	18 (tie)	70%
External Corporate			
● Sources of capital	13	14	71%
● Investor relations	19	20 (3 way tie)	50%
● Market analyst pressures	18	16	60%
● Political change	17	12	73%
● Regulatory change/compliance	8	8	69%
● Rating agency relations	25 (tie)	28	100%

Ranking based on weighted average score

Risk Sources and Treatment

13. For each of the following risk sources, please indicate how important the risk is to your organization (H=high, M=medium, L=low), whether you are actively managing the risk now and, if not, whether you plan to manage the risk within the next three years. Also, please indicate whether the risk source is factored into your ERM process.

With respect to each of the following risk sources:	How important is it? (H/M/L)	Percent actively managing it	Percent not managing it now who plan to manage it in the next three years	Percent indicating this risk source is factored into ERM process
Market				
• Inflation	2.31	28%	17%	27%
• Interest rate	3.58	73%	97%	43%
• Liquidity	3.47	80%	100%	51%
• Currency/Foreign exchange	2.69	60%	72%	30%
• Commodity prices	2.82	47%	45%	37%
• Asset market value	2.93	53%	56%	41%
• Share valuation	3.35	49%	43%	32%
• Capital markets	3.27	59%	54%	37%
• Reputation/rating	4.40	75%	100%	37%
Credit				
• Loan default	2.44	61%	55%	35%
• Counterparty credit	2.50	54%	48%	36%
• Exposure	2.93	64%	81%	45%
• Vendor risk	2.70	61%	73%	41%
Operational				
• People/intellectual capital	4.40	68%	100%	51%
• Business process changes brought about by e-business /Internet	3.85	66%	98%	47%
• Tort and contractual liability	3.12	68%	90%	47%
• Reinvestment	2.30	42%	32%	26%
• Technology	4.23	78%	100%	54%
• Competition	4.18	73%	100%	48%
• Natural disasters	2.32	60%	60%	48%
• Customer preferences	3.77	67%	77%	46%
• M&A integration	3.26	51%	38%	37%
• Distribution channels	3.17	54%	55%	38%

The Institute of Internal Auditors Research Foundation

With respect to each of the following risk sources:	How important is it? (H/M/L)	Percent actively managing it	Percent not managing it now who plan to manage it in the next three years	Percent indicating this risk source is factored into ERM process
• Expenses	4.04	81%	100%	57%
• Management effectiveness	3.96	58%	62%	44%
• Supplier problems	2.67	55%	59%	37%
• Products	3.55	64%	70%	39%
Political/Regulatory				
• Environment, health, and safety	3.43	68%	86%	47%
• Statutory liability	3.21	68%	90%	49%

14. Are the interactions (correlations, natural hedges, etc.) among the risk sources listed above factored into your:
   Assessment/measurement? (*Please choose one.*)
   42% Yes
   32 No
   21 Don't know
   5 No answer
   Mitigation and financing strategies/tactics? (*Please choose one.*)
   54% Yes
   22 No
   18 Don't know
   5 No answer

15. To what extent are risks discussed explicitly in your:
   Strategic planning (*Please choose one.*)
   33% High
   34 Medium
   24 Low
   8 Don't know

The Institute of Internal Auditors Research Foundation

Operational planning (*Please choose one.*)

33% High
38   Medium
21   Low
9   Don't know

Financial planning (*Please choose one.*)

46% High
33   Medium
15   Low
6   Don't know

Procedures and Tools

16. Which of the following risks are included in your internal auditing plan? (*Please choose all that apply.*)

    88% Financial risks (e.g., asset risks, liability risks)
    83   Operational risks (e.g., business risks, event risks)
    49   Strategic risks (e.g., management decisions)
    12   Other

17. In which functions does a formal risk identification and assessment process take place? (*Please choose all that apply.*)

    63% Finance
    31   Sales and Marketing
    21   Human Resources
    48   Operations
    31   Legal
    26   Procurement
    23   Other
    12   None at this time

18. For each of the risk management procedures listed below, please answer the following questions:

    (A) Do you consider the procedure important within your organization? (*Yes/No or Don't Know*)

    (B) Are you currently using this procedure? (*Yes/No or Don't Know*)

    (C) If not currently using, are you planning to implement this procedure within the next three years? (*Yes/No or Don't Know*)

Procedure	(A) Percent indicating important	(B) Percent currently using this procedure	(C) If not, percent planning to implement it within the next three years
18a. Conducting formal, enterprise-wide risk identification	82%	44%	72%
18b. Ranking the materiality of individual risks from an enterprise-wide perspective	86%	41%	70%
18c. Consolidating the ranking of disparate risks using a common metric	66%	24%	52%
18d. Incorporating formal risk assessment into the organization's due diligence process for mergers, acquisitions or major investments	74%	38%	60%
18e. Using probabilistic modeling techniques to measure relevant risks	48%	25%	35%
18f. Measuring the portfolio effect or diversification benefit of combining independent and/or negatively correlated risks (i.e., natural hedges)	55%	23%	35%
18g. Establishing capital requirements based on measurement of risks	65%	28%	45%
18h. Allocating capital to business segments based on measurement of risks	65%	25%	45%
18i. Evaluating the performance of your risk management strategies in light of your risk/return requirements	67%	24%	38%
18j. Using portfolio enhancement techniques	41%	18%	22%
18k. Incorporating risk management into your personnel management and/or executive compensation programs	63%	15%	36%

The Institute of Internal Auditors Research Foundation

Procedure	(A) Percent indicating important	(B) Percent currently using this procedure	(C) If not, percent planning to implement it within the next three years
18l. Implementing risk management programs through formal change management approaches	60%	21%	35%
18m. Exploiting integrated risk financing products (e.g., insurance/capital markets solutions)	55%	36%	36%
18n. Securitizing risk	45%	26%	33%
18o. Communicating risk assessments and responses to stakeholders	74%	43%	61%
18p. Communicating risk assessments and responses in the annual report	50%	21%	25%
18q. Devolving risk assessment and response duties to operating units	73%	41%	67%
18r. Using a coherent framework to guide the above activities	82%	36%	78%

The Institute of Internal Auditors Research Foundation

19. What tools do you typically use to help implement your risk management procedures? *(Please indicate by placing a "1" next to the primary tool(s) you use and a "2" by the secondary tool(s) you use.)*

Type of Tool	Primary tool(s)	Secondary tool(s)
Risk mapping of individual risks (e.g., using frequency /severity maps)	50%	9%
Risk assessment workshops	44	9
Economic scenario generation	10	18
Monte Carlo simulations	14	11
Catastrophe modeling	8	14
Scenario planning	20	19
Probabilistic (stochastic) simulation	11	13
Pro forma financial modeling	28	13
Optimization software	4	8
Management "dashboards"	15	6
Behavior modification performance incentives	9	10
Other	3	2

20. What metric(s) do you use to measure your ERM activities? *(Please indicate by placing a "1" next to the primary metric(s) you use and a "2" by the secondary metric(s) you use. You may indicate more than one primary and secondary metric as appropriate.)*

Type of Metric	Primary Metric(s)	Secondary Metric(s)
Cost of Risk (COR)	21%	3%
Value at Risk (VAR)	22	11
Risk Adjusted Return on Capital (RAROC)	12	8
Return on Capital Employed (ROC or ROCE)	18	6
Economic Value Added™ (EVA)	12	8
Mark-to-Market	17	5
Mark-to-Future™	2	2
Probability of Ruin	7	4
Expected Cost of Ruin	5	4
Below Target Risk	1	5
Earnings at Risk	11	10
Other	5	0
No metric currently being used	24	-

21. How do you communicate with key stakeholder groups about your risk management activities? *(Please choose all that apply.)*

28% Separate section devoted to risk management in the annual report
9   Continuing focus groups with key customers
8   Continuing focus groups with key suppliers
2   Continuing focus groups with local community/public
24   Provide separate information to security analysts/rating agencies
16   Other
29   Do not communicate with key stakeholders about risk management activities

The Institute of Internal Auditors Research Foundation

Company Profile

22. What type of company are you? *(Please choose all that apply.)*
    54% Public stock
    16   Private stock
    2   Mutual
    2   Mutual holding company
    1   Fraternal
    17   Other
    8   No answer

23. What is your primary industry classification? *(Please choose one.)*
    15% Energy and Mining
    12   Insurance
    12   Other Financial Services
    5   Healthcare
    13   Manufacturing
    8   Public Sector
    5   Retail
    4   Services
    6   Technology
    8   Telecommunications/Information Technology/Media/Entertainment
    2   Transportation
    5   Other
    5   No answer

24. What were your total revenues (U.S. dollars) in the most recently completed fiscal year?
    (Please choose one.)
    12% <$100 Million
    8    $100 – $249 Million
    8    $250 – $499 Million
    7    $500 – $999 Million
    31   $1 – $4.9 Billion
    15   $5 – $9.9 Billion
    7    $10 – $24.9 Billion
    5   >$25 Billion
    7   No answer

25. What were your total assets (U.S. dollars) in the most recently completed fiscal year? *(Please choose one.)*

    11% <$250 Million
    7    $250 – $499 Million
    9    $500 – $999 Million
    21   $1 – $4.9 Billion
    18   $5 – $14.9 Billion
    8    $15 – $24.9 Billion
    8    $25 – $39.9 Billion
    11   >$40 Billion
    7   No answer

26. What best describes the scope of your operations? *(Please choose one.)*

    43% Multinational/global
    2   Asia/Pacific
    1   Europe
    0   Latin America
    15   North America
    19   Presence limited to one country
    8   Presence limited to one territory
    4   Other
    9   No answer

APPENDIX III
THE VALUE OF CONSISTENCY

Background Information on Towers Perrin Consistency Analysis

Overview

Consistency analysis empirically estimates whether organizations with more consistent earnings receive a premium market valuation relative to peers. Since many other factors — in addition to earnings consistency — shape market valuations, we use a series of basic analytic steps to attempt to control for the influence of other factors (e.g., earnings growth and return on capital) and isolate a consistency premium or discount. We use a relatively simple control process since (1) we find that more complicated methods introduce other sources of "noise" into the process and (2) consistency premiums are fairly robust across many industry groups and emerge readily with relatively simple control techniques. A general description of the control process is provided below. For specific definitions and data sources used in the analysis, please see the Methodology section that follows.

Basic Methodology

In performing consistency analysis, Towers Perrin's first step is to identify a relevant industry peer sample for a given organization. Using an industry peer group helps filter out the effect of common industry factors (e.g., commodity price movements, regulatory risk) on market valuations. We typically use published industry groupings provided by ValueLine or Standard & Poors.

Next, we create a data set including a market premium measure, earnings growth rate, return on capital, and earnings consistency for each peer. We employ historical growth rates and returns as surrogates for the future growth rates and returns that drive valuations. We calculate growth rates, using a least squares (regression) approach to avoid biases caused by point-to-point methodology, and average returns on capital over the measurement window (typically ten years). To measure the market premium, we employ either a standardized market value-added metric or a market-to-book metric. We have had similar results using either metric. Finally, ValueLine's earnings predictability score (0-100 percent) is used as the measure of earnings consistency.

The Institute of Internal Auditors Research Foundation

We then calculate a median growth rate and return on capital for the peers and break the sample into four non-overlapping subsets: "low growth" (growth < median)/"low return" (return < median); "high growth"/"low return"; "low growth"/"high return"; and "high growth"/"high return." The process is repeated one more time by calculating the median earnings predictability score for each of the four subsets and then further breaking each subset into a high earnings consistency (earnings predictability >= subset median) and low earnings consistency (earnings predictability < subset median). A total of eight subsets result from both steps. The terms "low volatility" and "high volatility" are used interchangeably with the terms "high consistency" and "low consistency," respectively.

Finally, an average market premium (standardized market value added or market-to-book) is calculated for each of the eight subsets, and the results are summarized in bar chart form.

Towers Perrin Consistency Analysis Methodology

1. **Data Sources:**
   - *Compustat PC Plus database*
   - *ValueLine Investment Survey (Earnings consistency only)*

2. **Performance Metric Definitions:**

   A. **"Return on Capital"**
      - *Definition*
        – 10-year (1989-98) average Return on Capital Employed (ROCE)
      - *Formula*
        – (Income before Extraordinary Items + Special items)
          (Beginning Stockholders' Equity + Beginning Total Debt)
        – Perform same calculation for 10 years and take average
      - *Comment*
        – Simplified return on invested capital definition (provides some adjustment for restructuring charges and other one-offs but makes simplifying assumption that special items receive no tax deduction)
        – Note: Compustat does not report after-tax special items

B. "Earnings Growth"

- *Definition*
  - 10-year (1989-98) least-squares EBIT growth rate
- *Formula*
  - Regress log adjusted operating income after depreciation against time to determine growth rate
- *Comment*
  - Growth rate based on regression more accurate than CAGR (which is biased by end-points).

C. "Earnings Consistency"

- *Definition*
  - ValueLine Earnings Predictability score as reported in ValueLine Investment survey
- *Formula*
  - ValueLine earnings predictability scoring based on stability of year-to-year comparisons, with recent years being weighted more heavily than earlier ones. The earnings stability is derived from the standard deviation of the percentage changes in quarterly earnings over an eight-year period. Special adjustments are made for comparisons around zero and from plus to minus.

D. "Market Premium"

(Note: the market premium described below applies to standardized market value added, but could also be substituted with traditional market-to-book metric).

- *Definition*
  - 1998 Standardized Market Value Added (MVA) based on 1988 ending invested capital base
- *Formula*
  - Std MVA = MVA Percent Capital x Indexed Capital = (M/C - 1) x Indexed Capital
  - M/C = (Stock price * Common shares outstanding + Preferred stock +Total debt)/ (Shareholders' equity+Total debt)
    - All data reflect year-end 1998
  - Indexed Capital = (1998 Shareholders' equity+1998 Total debt)/(1988 Shareholders' equity+1988 Total debt)
- *Comment*
  - Market Value Added (MVA) captures value of growth (unlike M/B ratio) since it is measured in dollars. Standardizing MVA (by indexing every organization's capital to same base year) corrects size bias of measure (so big organizations with lots of capital but low M/C don't dominate smaller organizations with higher M/C).

APPENDIX IV
ENTERPRISE RISK MANAGEMENT
BIBLIOGRAPHY

The following is a list of representative sources for additional reading on the subject of Enterprise Risk Management.

Alexander, Carol, "Risk Management and Analysis," *Measuring and Modeling Financial Risk* (March 1999), 300 pp.

Andel, Tom, "Is Your Enterprise in Good Hands?," *Transportation & Distribution* (June 1999), p. SCF2.

Anonymous, "Competitive Strategies For a New Era," *Bank Systems & Technology* (August 1996), p. 48.

Anonymous, "Enterprise Risk Management Solution," *Wall Street & Technology* (October 1996), p. 81.

Anonymous, "Enterprise Risk Management: What's Driving The Trend?," *Financial Executive* (September/October 1998), p. 32.

Anonymous, "ERM a Priority Post Y2K, Spending on The Rise," *Wall Street & Technology* (July 1999), p. 114.

Anonymous, "Insurance Executives Need Better Enterprise Risk Management," *Community Banker* (May 2000), p. 42.

Anonymous, "Buying a Financial Umbrella," *The Economist* (June 2000), p. 75.

Anonymous, "A New World of Risks," *Best's Review Life Health Edition* (January 2000), p. 3.

Anonymous, "Insurance Broker Predicts Utility Trends," *Electric Light & Power* (June 1997), p. 8.

Anonymous, "Managing Risk - All On One Page," *Harvard Management Update* (Nov 1998), p. 12.

Anonymous, "Survey Of Risk Managers Reveals Dissatisfaction With Prioritizing Techniques," *Insurance Advocate* (May 2000), p. 18.

Anonymous, "Harvard Business Review on Managing Uncertainty," *Harvard Business School Press* (January 1999), 224 pp.

Anonymous, "Expanding the Envelope," *Business Insurance* (April 1999), p. 116.

Anonymous, "Treasury in an Uncertain World," *Treasury & Risk Management* (March 1999). Retrieved November 16, 2000. http://www.treasuryandrisk.com/html/Articles/TRM/1999/99Matrea.html,

Aon Risk Services, "Enterprise Risk Management: Part One," *Aon Insights* (Edition 3, 1999).

Aon Risk Services, "Enterprise Risk Management: Part Two," *Aon Insights* (Edition 4, 1999).

Aon Risk Services, "Investigating Enterprise Risk Management: Part One," *Aon Insights* (Edition 1, 2000).

Aon Risk Services, "Investigating Enterprise Risk Management: Part Two," *Aon Insights* (Edition 2, 2000).

Aon Risk Services, "Investigating Enterprise Risk Management: Part Three," *Aon Insights* (Edition 4, 2000).

Aon Risk Services, "Enterprise Risk Management," *Aon.com.* (Retrieved November 16, 2000). <http://www.aon.com/solutions/prod_serv/ps_28.asp>.

Aon Risk Services, "What is ERM?," *Aon.com.* (Retrieved November 16, 2000). <http://www.aon.com/solutions/prod_serv/ERM/erm1.asp>.

Aon Risk Services, "ERM Trends," Aon.com. (Retrieved November 16, 2000). <http://www.aon.com/solutions/prod_serv/ERM/erm2.asp>.

The Institute of Internal Auditors Research Foundation

Aon Risk Services., "ERM FAQ's: What's on The CEO's Mind When it Comes to Risk?," *Aon.com.* (Retrieved November 16, 2000). <http://www.aon.com/solutions/prod_serv/ERM/erm3.asp>.

Aon Risk Services, "ERM Solutions," *Aon.com.* (Retrieved November 16, 2000). <http://www.aon.com/solutions/prod_serv/ERM/erm4.asp>.

Aon Risk Services, "ERM Expert Profile: Another Perspective on Corporate Governance," *Aon.com.* (Retrieved November 16, 2000). <http://www.aon.com/solutions/prod_serv/ERM/erm9.asp>.

Arensman, Russ, "New Job Title: Chief Risk Officer," *Global Finance* (March 1998).

Arthus, Mark G., "Integrated Compliance and Total Risk Management: Creating a Bankwide Compliance System That Works," (McGraw-Hill, March 1994), 250 pp.

Banham, Russ, "Kit and Caboodle: Understanding The Skepticism About Enterprise Risk Management," *CFO Magazine* (April 1999), p. 63.

Banham, Russ, "Innovative Risk-Transfer Packages Aren't Making The Cut," *Treasury & Risk Management* (October 1999), p. 39.

Banham, Russ, "Street Fighters," *International Business* (September/October 1997), p. 19.

Banham, Russ, "Whatever The Weather: How United Grain Growers Tamed Mother Nature in Completing The Deal of The Decade," *CFO Magazine* (June 2000), p. 117.

Banham, Russ, "The Final Frontier of Risk," *ReActions* (May 1999), p. 20.

Banham, Russ, "Top Cops of Risk," *CFO Magazine* (September 2000), p. 91.

Beckstrom, Rod A., "Not Too Risky a Business," *The Banker* (July 1997), p. 90.

Berry, Andrew, and Julian Phillips, "Enterprise Risk Management: Pulling It Together," *Risk Management* (September 1998), p. 53.

Berry, Andrew, "Future Shock? An Industry Forecast," *Risk Management* (April 2000), p. 25.

Birkbeck, Kimberly, *Realizing The Rewards of Risk: How Integrated Risk Management Can Help Your Organization - Proceedings of The 1998 International Conference on Risk Management,* (Conference Board of Canada, April 1998).

Birkbeck, Kimberly, *Forewarned is Forearmed: Identification and Measurement in Integrated Risk Management,* (Conference Board of Canada, February 1999).

Birkbeck, Kimberly, *Integrating Risk Management: Strategically Galvanizing Resources in The Organization Proceedings of The 1998 International Conference on Risk Management,* (Conference Board of Canada, April 1998).

Borodovsky, Lev, *Practitioner's Handbook of Financial Risk Management,* (Butterworth-Heinemann, May 2000), 832 pp.

Bradford, Michael, "CRO Role Suited to Enterprise Risk Plans," *Business Insurance* (May 15, 2000), p. 16.

Bradford, Michael, "Definition Varies, But Enterprise Risk Cover Draws Interest," *Business Insurance* (November 13, 2000), p. 3.

Brown, Debra L., and David A.H. Brown, *Strategic Leadership for Effective Corporate Communications,* (The Conference Board of Canada Meeting Briefing, February 2000), 6 p.

Brown, Gregory W., "Mastering Risk: Seeking Security in a Volatile World," *Financial Times* (May 16, 2000).

Busman, Evan R., and Paul Van Zuiden, "The Challenge Ahead: Adopting an Enterprise-wide Approach to Risk," *Risk Management* (January 1998), p. 14.

Butterworth, Mark, "Mastering Risk: The Emerging Role of the Risk Manager," *Financial Times* (April 25, 2000).

Cannon, Tom, *A Guide to Integrated Risk Management,* (London: AIRMIC, 1999), 24 pp.

Carlson, Neil F., "Global Risk Management," *Strategic Finance* (August 1999) Retrieved November 27, 2000: <http://www.mamag.com/strategicfinance/1999/08j.htm>.

Challis, Simon, "An Enterprising View of Risk," *ReActions* (May 1999), p. 5.

Clark, Brent, "Enterprise Risk — What's Up With That?," *International Risk Management Institute* (October 2000), Retrieved December 5, 2000. <http://www.irmi.com/expert/articles/clark003.asp>.

Cohen, Michael, and Ron Crompton "Managing Risk Through an Enterprise Approach," *Mercer on Transport* (Fall/Winter 1999), p. 29.

Conley, John, "Multiple Lines: A Status Report on The Building Trend," *Risk Management* (January 2000), p. 19.

Conley, John, "Waves of the Future," *Risk Management* (July 1999), p. 13.

Conley, John, "3 Winning Ways," *Risk Management* (December 1999), p. 12.

Conn, Lowell, "Holistic Risk on The Horizon," *Canadian Underwriter* (June 1999), p. 12.

Cox, J.J., and N. Tait, *Reliability, Safety and Risk Management* (Butterworth-Heinemann, January 1991), 256 pp.

DeLoach, James, *Enterprise-Wide Risk Management*, (FT Prentice Hall, 1998), 284 pp.

Denning, Richard F., "Enterprise RM Must Start With The Data," *National Underwriter/Property & Casualty Edition* (June 5, 2000), p. 12.

Dickinson, Gerry, "Mastering Management: Risk Role Grows to Enterprise Scale," *Financial Times* (November 13, 2000).

Doherty, Neil A., *Integrated Risk Management: Techniques and Strategies for Managing Corporate Risk,* (McGraw Hill, 2000), 560 pgs.

Dowd, Kevin, *Beyond Value at Risk: The New Science of Risk Management,* (John Wiley & Sons, Inc., February 1998), 286 pp.

Dvorak, Phred, "Japan's Largest Insurer Loses $2 Billion in Gamble on Euro-Denominated Bonds," *The Wall Street Journal* (June 5, 2000), p. A22.

Eiss, Elizabeth, "Enterprising Solutions," *Risk Management* (August 1999), p. 34.

Elbert, Paul, "Safe and Sound," *American Gas* (September 1999), p. 24.

Ewing, Lace, "Don't Buy Anything Until You Talk to Your Risk Manager," *Treasury & Risk Management* (May/June 2000), p. 5.

Finger, Christopher C., and Allan M. Malz, "Mastering Risk: Welcome to This Week's One in a Million Event One-In-A-Million Event," *Financial Times* (June 6, 2000).

Fletcher, Lee, "Spencer Grants $300,000," *Business Insurance* (May 15, 2000), p. 1.

Fusaro, Peter C., *Energy Risk Management: Hedging Strategies and Instruments for the International Energy Markets,* (McGraw-Hill, April 2, 1998), 256 pp.

Gastineau, Gary L. and Mark P. Kritzman, *Dictionary of Financial Risk Management,* (Irwin Professional Pub., January 15, 1996), 307 pp.

Gjertsen, Lee Ann, "M&M Unit Tackles Enterprise Risk," *National Underwriter/Property & Casualty Edition* (April 3, 2000), p. 17.

Glasserman, Paul, "Mastering Risk: The Quest for Precision Through Value-at-Risk," *Financial Times* (May 16, 2000).

Global Assn. of Risk Professionals, "Chief Risk Officers - How Will Their New Role Change Finance?," *GARP Newsletter* (December 2000), Retrieved December 5, 2000. <http://www.garp.com/newsletters/dec2000.htm>.

Gruening, Hennie Van, *Analyzing Banking Risk: A Framework for Assessing Corporate Governance and Financial Risk Management,* (World Bank, April 1999), 289 pp.

Haimes, Yacov Y., *Risk Modeling, Assessment, and Management,* (Wiley-Interscience, August 1998), 688 pp.

Hanley, Mike, "Mastering Risk: Lowering Exposure by Spreading the Risk," *Financial Times* (May 2, 2000).

Harper, Kevin, "Saving Dollars by Managing Risk," *The American City & County* (April 1998), p. 8.

Hays, Daniel, "Risk Mgt. Consultants Focus on Offering Top-Down Programs," *National Underwriter/Property & Casualty Edition* (June 8, 1998), p. 3.

Hereth, Mark L., "Beyond The Box," *Risk Management* (March 1996), p. 29.

Hernandez, Luis Ramiro, "Integrated Risk Management in The Internet Age," *Risk Management* (June 2000), p. 29.

Herrick, R.C., "Exploring The Efficient Frontier," *Risk Management* (August 1997), p. 23.

Heywood, Derrick, "Foretelling The Future," *Australian CPA* (August 2000), p. 44.

Hoffman, Thomas, "Systems Deliver Functionality But Falter on Integration," *Computerworld* (February 10, 1997), p. 57.

Hovey, Juan, "Risky Business," *Industry Week* (May 15, 2000), p. 75.

Hulihan, Maile, "Enterprise-Wide Needs," *Treasury & Risk Management* (July 1999).

Jorion, Philippe, "Mastering Risk: Value, Risk and Control: A Dynamic Process in Need of Integration," *Financial Times* (May 16, 2000).

Katz, David M., "Business-risk Talk Spawns Little Action," *National Underwriter/Property & Casualty Edition* (May 11, 1998), p. 25.

Katz, David M., "Firm Touts 'Enterprise Risk Management,'" *National Underwriter/Property & Casualty Edition* (June 23, 1997), p. 19.

Katz, David M., "Insurers Seen Stalling Enterprise Risk Management," *National Underwriter/ Property & Casualty Edition* (April 10, 2000), p. 9.

Katz, David M., "CRO Career Dream Alive Among RMs," *National Underwriter/Property & Casualty Edition* (May 17, 1999), p. 25.

Katz, David M., "How Much of 'Operational' Risk Management is Hype?," *National Underwriter/Property & Casualty Edition* (June 5, 2000), p. 15.

Katz, David M., "Insurance Executives Doubt Their RM Abilities," *National Underwriter/Property & Casualty Edition* (May 29, 2000), p. 15.

Katz, David M., "RM Successes Called Career Launch Pad," *National Underwriter/Property & Casualty Edition* (February 14, 2000), p. 19.

Keaveney, Cindy, "Human Capital Also an Enterprise Risk," *Business Insurance* (January 1, 2001), p. 8.

Kendall, Robin, *Risk Management For Executives*, (FT Prentice Hall, 1998), 252 pp.

Khwaja, Amir, "Enterprise-wide Risk Management and the Impact of XML," *Erisk* (February 17, 2000), Retrieved December 5, 2000.
<http://www.erisk.com/reference/archive/ref_archive_ent_002.asp>.

Kielmas, Maria, "Enterprise Risk Management Utilized: Competitive Market Means Power Companies Must Consider New Exposures," *Business Insurance* (August 2, 1999), p. 35.

Kloman, Felix H., "Integrated Risk Assessment: Current Views of Risk Management," *Risk Management Reports* (April 1998), p. 2.

Kloman, Felix H., "Integrating Risk Management," *Risk Management Reports* (April 1997), p. 2.

Kloman, Felix H., "Internal Auditors," *Risk Management Reports* (November 1999), p. 2.

Knight, Rory, and Deborah Pretty, "Mastering Risk: Philosophies of Risk, Shareholder Value and the CEO," *Financial Times* (June 27, 2000).

Koritzinsky, Arthur, "'Enterprise Risk Management' Fuels Captive Surge," *National Underwriter/Property & Casualty Edition* (October 26, 1998), p. S21.

Kranhold, Kathryn, and Erin White, "The Perils and Potential Rewards of Crisis Managing for Firestone," *The Wall Street Journal* (September 8, 2000), p. B1.

Lam, James C., "Enterprise-wide Risk Management and the Role of the Chief Risk Officer," *ERisk* (March 25, 2000), Retrieved November 27, 2000.
<http://www.erisk.com/reference/archive/ref_archive_ent_011.asp>.

Lam, James C., "Enterprise-wide Risk Management: Staying Ahead of the Convergence Curve," *Journal of Lending & Credit Risk Management* (June 1999), p. 16.

Lam, James C., "A New Role: Chief Risk Officer," *Business Journal* (November/December 1999), p. 55.

Lam, James C., "The CRO Is Here to Stay," *Risk Management* (April 2001), pp. 17-22.

Lam, James C., and Brian M. Kawamoto, "Emergence of The Chief Risk Officer," *Risk Management* (September 1997), p. 30.

Lange, Scott, "Going 'Full Bandwidth' at Microsoft," *Risk Management* (July 1996), p. 29.

Lee, Charles R., "Chief Risk Officer Stepping Up," *Risk Management* (September 2000), p. 22.

Lenkus, Dave, "Public Entity Adopts Holistic Plan: Enterprising Risk Manager," *Business Insurance* (January 1, 2001), p. 1.

Levin, Michael R., and Michael L. Rubenstein, "A Unique Balance: The Essence of Risk Management," *Risk Management* (September 1997), p. 37.

Levine, Harvey A., "Risk is a Four-Letter Word, But Denial is our Biggest Enemy," White Paper, (Scitor Corp., Retrieved November 16, 2000). <http://www.scitor.com/resources/white_papers/Riskpuzl.htm>.

Levinsohn, Alan, "A Generation of Risk Managers Fortell a Future," *ABA Banking Journal* (October 1998), p. 74.

Lo, Andrew W., "The Three P's of Total Risk Management," *Financial Analysts Journal* (January/February 1999), p. 13.

Lutkins, Clint, "Integrated Risk Programs Gain Ground," *Canadian Underwriter* (April 2000), p. 22.

Marjanovic, Steven, "Ex-Bankers Trust President Starts Risk Management Firm," *American Banker* (June 18, 1997), p. 18.

Marlin, Steven, "Risk Management: Banks Wager on Enterprise Systems," *Bank Systems & Technology* (September 1998), p. 30.

Marray, Michael, "Insurers Put Pressure on Capital Markets," *Airfinance Journal* (September 1999), p. 22.

Marray, Michael, "Risk Becomes More Enterprising," *Airfinance Journal* (December 1998), p. 28.

Martin, Pamela, and Kathleen M. Beans, "Enterprise-wide Risk Management," *Journal of Lending & Credit Risk Management* (March 2000), p. 22.

McDonald, Lee, "Ryan's Hope: Change and More Change," *Best's Review Life/Health Insurance Edition* (March 1998), p. 84.

McEachern, Christina, "Crystal Box Offers Clear View of Risk Management at CDC," *Wall Street & Technology* (March 2000), p. 64.

McEachern, Christina, "Risk: Enterprise-wide Risk Technology Spending Reaches a Plateau, Credit Still Rising," *Wall Street & Technology* (October 1, 2000), p. 54.

McEachern, Cristina, "Risk Management Tech Spending on the Rise," *Wall Street & Technology* (Fourth Quarter 1999), p. 7.

McEachern, Cristina, "Risk Vendors Jump on The Buy-side Bandwagon," *Wall Street & Technology* (Fourth Quarter 1999), p. 16.

McGinn, Carol, "The New Risk Management," *Wall Street & Technology* (July 1998), p. 88.

McIntyre, Kathryn J., "A Risk Approach For The Enterprising," *Business Insurance* (October 18, 1999), p. 61.

McLeod, Douglas, "New Chief Risk Officer Role Coordinates Risk Strategy," *Business Insurance* (April 26, 1999), p. 3.

McLeod, Douglas, "Enterprise Risk Policy Crafted," *Business Insurance* (January 31, 2000), p. 2.

McNamee, David, and Georges Selim, *Risk Management: Changing The Internal Auditor's Paradigm*, (Altamonte Springs, FL, The Institute of Internal Auditors Research Foundation, 1998), 219 pp.

McNamee, David, *Business Risk Assessment,* (Altamonte Springs, FL, The Institute of Internal Auditors Research Foundation, 1998), 107 pp.

Melchers, R.E., *Integrated Risk Assessment: Applications and Regulations,* (Newcastle, Australia, May 1998), 140 pp.

Merkley, Brian W., "Does Enterprise Risk Management Count?," *Risk Management* (April 2001), pp. 25-28.

Meulbroek, Lisa, and Jonathan Barnett, "Honeywell, Inc. and Integrated Risk Management," *Harvard Business School Case* (July 12, 2000), 22 pp.

Meulbroek, Lisa, "Mastering Risk: Total Strategies for Company-Wide Risk Control," *Financial Times* (May 9, 2000).

Meulbroek, Lisa, "A Better Way to Manage Risk," *Harvard Business Review* (February 2001).

Miccolis, Jerry A., "All Together Now," *Best's Review* (February 2000), p. 122.

Miccolis, Jerry A., "Enterprise Risk Management: What's Beyond The Talk?," (International Risk Management Institute, May 2000). <http://www.irmi.com/expert/articles/miccolis001.asp>.

Miccolis, Jerry A., "Enterprise Risk Management in the Financial Services Industry: Still a Long Way To Go," (International Risk Management Institute, August 2000). Retrieved December 5, 2000. http://www.irmi.com/expert/articles/miccolis002.asp

Miccolis, Jerry A., "Toward a Universal Language of Risk," *Risk Management* (July 1996), p. 45.

Miccolis, Jerry A., "Enterprise Risk Management in the Financial Services Industry: From Concept to Management Process," (International Risk Management Institute, November 2000). Retrieved December 5, 2000. <http://www.irmi.com/expert/articles/miccolis003.asp>

Miccolis, Jerry A., and Samir Shah, "Enterprise Risk Management: An Analytic Approach," *Tillinghast – Towers Perrin Monograph,* (January 2000), 36 pp.

Miccolis, Jerry A., and Samir Shah, "RiskValueInsights™: Creating Value through Enterprise Risk Management – A Practical Approach for the Insurance Industry," *Tillinghast – Towers Perrin Monograph,* (June 2001), 94 pp.

Miccolis, Jerry A., and Samir Shah, "RiskValueInsights™: Creating Value through Enterprise Risk Management – A Practical Approach for the Insurance Industry," *Tillinghast – Towers Perrin Executive Brief,* (April 2001), 10 pp.

Miccolis, Jerry A., and Samir Shah, "Risk Management: Getting a Handle on Operational Risks," *Emphasis* (2000/1), p. 22.

Miccolis, Jerry A., and Timothy P. Quinn, "What's Your Appetite For Risk? Determining The Optimal Retention," *Risk Management* (April 1996), p. 41.

Mitroff, Ian, "The Essentials of Crisis Management," *Financial Times* (June 20, 2000), p. 4.

Molnar, Michele, "More Companies Embrace Enterprise Risk Management," *Office.com.* (May 10, 2000). Retrieved November 20, 2000. <http://www.office.com/search/office.com/article?ARTICLE=17663>.

Moules, Jonathan, "The Next Frontier," *Treasury & Risk Management* (July 1999). Retrieved December 9, 2000. <http://www.treasuryandrisk.com/html/Articles/TRM/1999/99JLthen.html>.

Mullins, Ronald Gift, "People Issues Are Firms' Top Risk," *Journal of Commerce* (May 30, 2000), p. 8.

Nottingham, Lucy, *A Conceptual Framework for Integrated Risk Management*, (Conference Board of Canada, September 1997), 4 pp.

O'Sullivan, Orla, "Countering The Domino Effect," *U.S. Banker* (August 1999), p. 44.

Pelland, Dave, "Greater Emphasis on Financial Skills: Changing Face of Risk Management," *Risk Management* (April 1997), p. 108.

Phipps, Joel, "Integrating Financial, Insurance Risks Takes Team Effort," *National Underwriter/ Property & Casualty Edition* (October 26, 1998), p. S32.

Price, Margaret, "Under Control," *Treasury & Risk Management* (October 1998), p. 30.

PricewaterhouseCoopers, *The Regulatory Risk Management Handbook: 1998-1999,* (Sharpe, M.e., Inc., September 1998), 208 pp.

Prince, Michael, "ERM RMIS Requires Corporate Cultural Transformation," *Business Insurance* (December 4, 2000), p. 21.

Punter, Alan, "The Changing Economics of Non-Life Insurance: New Solutions for the Financing of Risk," *White Paper, Aon Group Limited* (March 29, 2000), 23 pp.

Quinn, Lawrence Richter, "Enterprise Risk: All Wrapped Up To Go," *Risk & Insurance* (October 1, 1999), p. 1.

Quinn, Lawrence Richter, "The Ever-Widening Spectrum of Risk," *Risk and Insurance* (October 1, 2000), p. 43.

Rahardjo, Kay, and Mary Ann Dowling, "A Broader Vision: Strategic Risk Management," *Risk Management* (September 1998), p. 44.

Rastallis, Jane Y., and Jerry A. Miccolis, "Risk Managing Shareholder Value," *Emphasis* (1999/3), p. 18.

Roberts, Sally, "Top Priority on Bottom Line," *Business Insurance* (March 20, 2000), p. 3.

Roberts, Sally, "Interest Wanes in Earnings Cover: Policy Takes Downhill Turn," *Business Insurance* (December 11, 2000), p. 1.

Riggins, Donald J. "So You Want to be a Chief Risk Officer?," *Financing Risk & Reinsurance*, pp. 8-11.

Sanderson, Scott M., and Arthur G. Koritzinsky, "Risk Centers: Enterprise-Wide Efficiency," *Risk Management* (March 1999), p. S6.

Scherzer, Martin H., "Earnings Insurance: Mission Impossible?." *Financial Executive* (May/June 1999), p. 53.

Scherzer, Martin H., "Risky Business," *Financial Executive* (Sep/Oct 1998), p. 30.

Schneier, Robert, and Jerry A. Miccolis, "Enterprise Risk Management," *Strategy & Leadership* (March/April 1998), p. 10.

Seuntjens, Thomas, "Look, Boss I Cut the Premiums!," *Treasury & Risk Management* (January/February 2000), p. 8.

Slywotzky, Adrian, James A. Quella, and David J. Morrison, "Countering Strategic Risk With Pattern Thinking," *Mercer Management Journal* (November 1999), p. 11.

Souter, Gavin, "New Marsh Enterprise Unit to Focus on Integrated Risks," *Business Insurance* (March 27, 2000), p. 1.

Souter, Gavin, "Managing Risk Adds Value," *Business Insurance* (October 30, 2000), p. 2.

Spinner, Karen, "Pulling It All Together," *Wall Street & Technology* (Fourth Quarter 1999), p. 7.

Spinner, Karen, "Hedging Credit, Market Risk," *Wall Street & Technology* (Spring 1998), p. 23.

Stavros, Richard, "Risk Management: Where Utilities Still Fear to Tread," *Public Utilities Fortnightly* (October 15, 2000), p. 40.

Stulz, Rene, "Mastering Risk: Diminishing the Threats to Shareholder Wealth," *Financial Times* (April 25, 2000).

Talmor, Sharona, "Technotes," *Banker* (March 1998), p. 74.

Teach, Edward, "Microsoft's Universe of Risk," *CFO Magazine* (March 1997).

Thornhill, Wil and Amy Derksen, "A United Approach: Creating Integrated Risk Plans," *Risk Management* (August 1998), p. 36.

Tillinghast – Towers Perrin, "Enterprise Risk Management in The Insurance Industry: 2000 Benchmarking Survey Report," (2000), 29 pp.

Treasury Board of Canada Secretariat, "Best Practices in Risk Management: Private and Public Sectors Internationally," Retrieved November 17, 2000. <http://www.tbs-sct.gc.ca/pubs_pol/dcgpubs/riskmanagement/rm-pps_e.html>.

Veysey, Sarah, "'Holistic' View Debated: Few Products For Transferring Broad Array of Risk," *Business Insurance* (June 5, 2000), p. 33.

White, Leslie, and Melanie Herman, *Leaving Nothing to Chance: Achieving Board Accountability through Risk Management,* (National Center for Nonprofit Boards, October 1998), 32 pp.

Whitney, Sally, "Managing Internal Risks," *Best's Review* (April 2000), p. 141.

Williams, Deborah, "Choosing an ERM System That Suits Your Bank's Needs," *Bank Accounting & Finance* (Fall 1999), p. 39.

Williams, Todd L., "An Integrated Approach to Risk Management," *Risk Management* (July 1996), p. 22.

Williams, Todd L., "Convergence," *Risk Management* (August 1999), p. 13.

Young, Peter C., and Steven C. Tippins, *Managing Business Risk: An Organization-Wide Approach to Risk Management*, (AMACOM, September 2000), 256 pp.

Young, Peter C., and Martin Fone, "Organization Risk Management in UK Police Authorities: An Integrated Management Approach," (*White Paper. University of St. Thomas*). Retrieved November 16, 2000. <http:www.gsb.stthomas.edu/risk/police.htm>.

Zaffino, Jonathan M., "Expanding Risks: Enterprise Risk Management Solutions," *The John Liner Review* (Spring 2000), p. 63.

Zarb, Frank G., "Brokers at The Helm: Navigating The Risk Financing Frontier," *Risk Management* (July 1995), p. 53.

Zask, Ezra, *Global Investment Risk Management,* (McGraw-Hill, September 1999), 300 pp.

Zolkos, Rodd, "Enterprise, Integrated Programs Expand Choices," *Business Insurance* (November 15, 1999), p. 50.

Zolkos, Rodd, "Insurers Stymied in Managing Enterprise Risk," *Business Insurance* (April 17, 2000), p. 1.

Zolkos, Rodd, "Integrated Products Support Expanded Risk Manager Duties," *Business Insurance* (April 26, 1999), p. 3.

Zolkos, Rodd, "Balance Sheet Risks," *Business Insurance* (April 26, 1999), p. 36.

Zolkos, Rodd, "Enterprise Risk Management: Number of Chief Risk Officers Grows as Concept Takes Hold," *Business Insurance* (September 25, 2000), p. 3.

IIA Research Foundation
Board of Research Advisors
2000/2001

Chairman

Stephen A. Doherty, CPA, CISA, *Credit Lyonnais Americas*

Members

Charles H. "Bud" Allen, CBA, CISA, *Wilmington Trust Company*
Betty Ann Blandon, CIA, CPA, *RadioShack Corporation*
Joseph Vincent Carcello, PhD, CIA, CPA, CMA, *University of Tennessee*
Ali Akbar Chaudhry, *Pakistan*
Angelina K. Y. Chin, CIA, CPA, CISA, CBA, *General Motors Company*
Michel Doyon, CIA, *Bell Canada*
Gareth Evans, MIIA, *United Kingdom*
John M. Furka, CPA, *Brown Brothers Harriman & Co.*
Kasey K. Kiplinger, CIA, CGFM, *Iowa Workforce Development Administration Center*
Gary J. Mann, PhD, CPA, *University of Texas at El Paso*
Steven S. Mezzio, CIA, *PricewaterhouseCoopers LLP*
John R. Mills, PhD, CPA, *University of Nevada*
Jane F. Mutchler, PhD, CPA, *Georgia State University*
Claire Beth Nilsen, CRCM, CFE, CFSA, *Philadelphia Stock Exchange*
Heriot Calder Prentice, *IIA UK & Ireland*
Mark R. Radde, CIA, CPA, *Buffets, Inc.*
Kathy B. Robinson, CIA, *Morgan Stanley Dean Witter*
Mark L. Salamasick, CISA, CDP, CSP, *Bank of America*
Clarence O. Smith, CIA, CISA, *C.O. Smith and Associates*
Frank Robert Tallerico, CIA, CPA, *Pioneer Hi Bred International, Inc.*
James H. Thompson, CIA, *James Thompson & Associates*
Curtis C. Verschoor, PhD, CIA, CMA, CPA, CFP, *DePaul University*
Scott D. White, CIA, CBA, CISA, CTA, *Sun Life of Canada*

IIA Staff Liaison

Susan B. Lione, CIA, CCSA, *Senior Manager of Research*

The Institute of Internal Auditors Research Foundation

IIA RESEARCH FOUNDATION

Chairman's Circle

AT&T
Cargill, Inc.
Entergy Services, Inc.
General Motors Corporation
J.C. Penney Company, Inc.
Microsoft Corporation
PepsiCo, Inc.
PricewaterhouseCoopers LLP
Southern Company Services, Inc.

The Institute of Internal Auditors Research Foundation